The Servant-Steward's Handbook

A Practical Guide to Effective Leadership and Supervision in Business or Ministry

Larry N. Gay and Susan T. Gay

The Servant-Steward's Handbook:
A Practical Guide to Effective Leadership and Supervision
in Business or Ministry

LEAD360, LLC
Montgomery, Alabama
Email: LEAD360@gmail.com

"First, I would say that this book is one of the best books on Christian leadership I have seen. As a Christian-foundational book it is faithful to the scriptures and filled with every possible Christian principle. You have done a good job throughout the book showing that Christian principles are just a significant and valuable in the secular workplace as in Christian contexts.

"Second, there have been previous efforts to write specifically on "supervision" due to the tremendous need then and today for good supervision among our own people. I have not found those sources very valuable. This book places "supervision" in the overall context of leadership development which is where it should be. In that light, it may be the best source available for developing supervisors in any organization and especially Christian organizations.

"Third, the book strikes a healthy balance between an academic approach and a practical approach to instruction. By that I mean it is challenging in its scholarship and easy to understand in its practicality. Striking this balance is not easy. This means it is mentally stimulating and easy to read and set goals to apply!
(Sam James, IMB, founder of the International Learning Center)

"What I appreciated about this book was the authors' use of the Biblical narrative for every principle they are promoting. I have read many leadership books and I found so many of them just being more like "recipe books" with an occasional verse to give it a "spiritual flavor." I found The Servant-Steward's Handbook to be based on Biblical values and principles that are the foundation for the practical methodology.

"I hope young leaders who read this book will take the time, not just to read the book and the references, but to actually study the context on which these values and

principles are built so they can take personal ownership of what the Handbook is saying.

"I wish I had this book almost 50 years ago when I got involved in leadership in our mission organization. It would have saved me from a multitude of headaches, and it would have equipped me well in my leadership responsibilities."
(Oli Jacobsen, Ethnos360)

To our three sons, Brian, Robert and Eric,
our pride and joy!

Acknowledgments

We could never give an adequate acknowledgment or expression of gratitude to everyone who has had an influence in the development of this handbook. Over the course of years, we have learned from mentors, supervisors, colleagues, friends, conference leaders, and long conversations with anyone who was interested in the subject of leadership development and supervision. Thank you to all of you and forgive us for not being able to list all of you by name.

Thanks to Sam James, Lloyd Rodgers, Van Payne, Tom Williams, Dickie Nelson and Elbert Smith for all their years of experience and their deep insights that emerged from our group exegetical study to form the biblical foundation for this handbook.

Thank you to the several friends who read early manuscripts or sat in our workshops and offered insights and suggestions for improvements—especially Todd Lafferty, Don Dent and Duane Ostrem.

Our friends John Bell, Jr. and John Bell, III gave insights from a business perspective and encouraged us to "go public" with what we had written. We do indeed hope this handbook becomes a practical desktop reference for people who want to be like you in their businesses.

Finally, to our editor, Joi Soo Tribble, thank you for the many hours and detailed markings that took our words to another level of excellence and professionalism that will make this handbook even more practical for leaders in business or ministry.

The Servant-Steward's Handbook
A Practical Guide to Effective Leadership and Supervision
in Business or Ministry

Contents

vii

Preface

In our years of leadership and followership we have observed leaders who were successful in their businesses and who had very high retention/very low attrition among their employees or teams. One of the most important things all of these effective leaders had in common was that they all held a very high value for the people with whom they worked and these people knew that they were valued. They all understood the counsel of King Rehoboam's senior advisors: *"If today you will be a servant to these people and serve them...they will always be your servants."* (1 Kings 12:7)

We have seen churches and other faith-based entities turn to secular business consultants to help them restructure their organizations on a corporate model. The results in almost every case have been decline in morale, reduced effectiveness, and eventually a turnover in core leadership—in a word, failure. Often the changes were focused on a monetary bottom line and did not give adequate consideration to how important the organization's personnel are to the fulfillment of the purpose, vision, and mission of that organization. We propose that, instead of churches and faith-based organizations looking to the corporate world for advice on how to do business, the corporate world ought to be asking Christian leaders to show them the way to excellence and success in fulfilling their purpose. Christian leaders are called to a higher standard that comes from an unwavering reliance on and practice of the principles found in the Word of God. As followers of Jesus, we are supposed to be salt and light for the rest of the world. (Mt.5:13-16)

Many Christian business men and women are asking, "Is it possible to be successful in business while abiding by the law and still being true to biblical principles?" We firmly believe the answer is *yes,* although we recognize that it is becoming more challenging every day. The principles of good leadership and supervision are applicable in any business, industry, or ministry and in any culture. While it is true that there will be many times when biblical principles come in direct confrontation with accepted societal norms, it is possible to do as Jesus said and *"render to Caesar the things that are Caesar's and to God the things that are God's."* (Mt.22:21)

We lived in Mexico City in 1985 when a giant earthquake brought down thousands of buildings killing as many as 20,000 people. Our neighbor, Rafael, was an architect and taught architecture in the National University there. In a society where corruption, bribery, and corner-cutting were the acceptable norm, Rafael taught his students that it was possible to build a safe structure in compliance with the law and building codes without paying any bribes—and also still make a profit. When he returned from his first survey of the damage after the earthquake, I (Larry) noticed that Rafael was emotionally shaken. I asked how many of his buildings had collapsed. None, he said, but at least one fellow architect whose buildings all fell causing significant loss of life had committed suicide jumping off one of Rafael's buildings that was structurally sound. Unlike his distressed colleague, Rafael felt very strongly that he had a stewardship responsibility to design and oversee the building of safe structures that would serve and protect many people for many years. He felt responsible for helping his students to catch that same vision, even if it meant having to swim upstream against the societal norm.

Whether you are a team leader, shift manager, sales executive, school principal, pastor, CEO of a Fortune 500 company, or a leader of volunteer teams, you have been given a stewardship responsibility to help others to be effective in their work and to feel they are contributing to something that helps fulfill their sense of purpose in life. Following the principles outlined in this handbook will help you do just that.

Most of the chapters have grown out of leadership development and team-building workshops we have led over the past 30 years. The workshops grew largely out of our own experiences, including those we learned from our mistakes, and the needs of the teams with which we have worked. Much of that experience has been in cross-cultural settings, so these principles should also be relevant to the specific challenges of supervising cross-cultural teams and teams that are separated by long distances.

This work is a partnership effort that we have worked on together. Many of the concepts were thrashed out on early morning or late evening walks or long drives. We have co-facilitated most of the workshops together. Whenever a personal illustration uses the pronoun "I," it is Larry talking. Otherwise, it really is "we."

Our hope is that this *Servant-Steward's Handbook* will be a practical desktop reference for anyone who supervises the work of others in any setting. Whether you are a novice manager or a seasoned veteran leader, we will keep reminding you that your leadership responsibility is really a *stewardship* responsibility. We hope some of the suggestions in this handbook will help you to be a more effective *servant-steward* of the people you have been entrusted to lead.

Larry Gay and Susan Gay
www.MyLEAD360.com
LEAD360@gmail.com
November 2019

How to Read This Book

This handbook is intended to be a practical reference guide for leaders or supervisors. It can be read sequentially or by topics as needed using the Table of Contents. Throughout the handbook, principles or characteristics of servant-stewards from the Pastoral Letters of the Apostle Paul to Timothy and Titus will be highlighted in a shaded text box. We have also included other biblical texts that provide additional foundations for the principles and practical applications of servant-stewardship. A summary list of the "Principles and Characteristics of the Servant-Steward" is included in the Appendix at the end of this handbook.

"The Servant-Steward Coaching Guide" (mentioned in the chapter on "Dialoguing for Development" and included in the Appendix) is a direct outgrowth from 2 Timothy 4:5 and can be as applicable in a secular workplace as it is in a ministry leadership evaluation. Two versions are included in this handbook with only a slight change in wording: one for ministry leaders and one for business leaders.

A number of practical tools and forms are included in the Appendix as a handy reference guide. These can be freely copied for your use in your business or ministry.

PART TWO includes the notes from the group exegesis as a commentary on the three letters to Timothy and Titus. We encourage you to study these letters and discover for yourself how relevant they are today even as they were to Paul, Timothy, and Titus in the first century.

PART ONE

Introduction to Servant-Stewardship

Although the "Pastoral Letters" of the Apostle Paul do not constitute a book on leadership, as such, these personal letters from the older experienced leader contain a wealth of instruction to two young leaders. Paul used these letters to mentor and advise Timothy and Titus from a distance without the benefit of the internet or electronic devices to connect in real time!

A small group of long-term veteran colleagues gathered to study these three letters (1 Timothy, 2 Timothy, and Titus) with the goal of defining a biblical basis to describe the character and characteristics of supervisors working with expatriate and cross-cultural teams. For twelve weeks, we met weekly to read through the entire text of the three letters in a group exegesis.

We were looking for a strong biblical and theological foundation for the selection, training, and evaluation of supervisors. What we discovered was a very effective leadership training manual that had already been compiled within Paul's letters. The group's exegesis of the three letters as one body pointed to multiple principles that good supervisors follow. Some of these principles are drawn from Paul's instructions and advice to Timothy and Titus. Others are derived from Paul's personal declarations about himself as a fellow servant who was demonstrating the stewardship responsibilities he felt for his young mentees. Many of the principles refer to all believers. Some are aimed specifically at leaders.

We discovered very practical, relevant principles for dealing with the issues that leaders in any organization face. Some of these include selecting good people, evaluating their work, dealing with difficult people, handling criticism, leading multi-generational teams, building unity, and more.

From a leadership perspective, these letters could not be more relevant for training effective leaders today. In our first session together, we only got through the first eleven verses of First Timothy and came up with eleven characteristics, which, we agreed, seem to point to the need for a new paradigm of leadership. Our conviction continued to grow as we continued our study.

The Need for a New Paradigm

Paradigms come and go. Today's new, cutting edge, innovative idea will become tomorrow's stodgy, old-fashioned, obsolete way of thinking. Although the ecclesiastical writing is true that that there is nothing entirely new under the sun (Ecc. 1:9-10), at the same time God clearly advocates our finding new ways to see the things He has provided for us from the beginning. We are called to sing a new song (Ps. 33:3; 40:3; 81:3; 96:1: 98:1; 144:9; 149:1; Is. 42:10); Jesus reminded us not to use new cloth to mend old clothing and to put new wine in new wineskins. (Lk. 5:36-39) He gave us a new commandment (Jn. 13:34) and a new covenant (Lk. 22:20) and He introduced a new teaching that was contrary to the way the religious leaders had been instructing people. (Mk. 1:27)

New paradigms are often an attempt to get back to the original way things were meant to be. Radical change is often necessary to return to the original intent and address the root of the problem. The study of Scripture often leads to a radical change of paradigms. A perfect example of this is found in 2 Kings 22-23 when Josiah led the people back to obedience of God through the reading, hearing, and application of the Word. This was also the case in the way Jesus taught in contrast to the styles of teachers and leaders of His time. He was drawing people back to the way He had intended the world to operate from its beginning and that required a radical change in the way people thought about their relationship to God and to each other—getting back to the way things were meant to be.

So, it should not be surprising that the group's exegesis of Paul's letters to Timothy and Titus would lead to a new way of looking at leadership and supervision. As the group studied the three letters, we were continually impressed with the relevance of the principles that surfaced and the need for a paradigm of leadership that would return to these timeless truths. This new paradigm can best be described as *servant-stewardship*.

Servant-stewards see their role as more than a job—it is a calling.

- Servant-stewards understand their stewardship responsibility that comes from God by faith. (1 Tim. 1:1-4; 4:14)
- Servant-stewards should be chosen based on clear evidence of God's call in their lives. (1 Tim. 1:12-17)
- Servant-stewards are chosen because others recognize the Spirit-given gift in them. (1 Tim. 4:14)
- When an individual is named to a place of leadership, it should not be surprising to those who have known them. (1 Tim. 1:18; 1 Tim. 3:10; Titus 1:5-9)
- Servant-stewards are respected by others. (1 Tim. 3:13)

Why Servant-Stewardship?

You might be asking, "What is so different about *servant-stewardship* from other leadership paradigms? Doesn't *servant-steward* mean the same thing as *servant-leader* or *leader-steward*?" Although the differences might seem subtle at first, the implications that emerge from the study of the Pastoral Letters seem to demand an adjustment in how we view the role and responsibilities of leadership and supervision.

Servant-stewardship emphasizes two key aspects of leadership. As a fellow *servant*, you recognize that you, like those you are tasked with leading, are also under authority. As a *steward*, you accept the responsibility given by those in authority over you to care for the people who have been placed within your sphere of influence. This includes the stewardship of relationships along with the gifts and strengths of each person.

Servant

Paul referred to himself as a servant of God. (Titus 1:1) The Greek word *doulos* is usually translated "servant," but it is probably more accurately translated as "bondservant" or "slave." Jesus used two words in Matthew 20:26-27 to describe the role his disciples are to take—*diakonos* and *doulos*. Jesus insisted that his followers were not to be like secular rulers who lord it over those they lead: *"It shall not be so among you. But whoever would be great among you must be your servant (diakonos), and whoever would be first among you must be your slave (doulos)."* (Mt.20:26-27)

Jesus set the example for this model of leading by serving. Paul described Jesus as having taken the role of *doulos,* a slave (Phil. 2:5-11) which He did most graphically the night before his crucifixion when He washed the feet of his disciples. (Jn. 13:1-20)

Steward

The concept of stewardship is an ancient one. The Greek term, *oikonomos,* describes a servant given responsibility over the household and/or finances of the owner as an overseer. The *oikonomos* could be either a slave or a free man who was voluntarily indentured to the owner. This word can be translated as manager, steward, or treasurer, all of which indicate a person who has been given a responsibility of leadership.

Stewardship as a leadership function can be traced all the way back to the very beginnings of humanity. In Genesis 2, God gave Adam specific responsibilities to watch over and care for the Garden of Eden as both gardener and guardian. Joseph was sold into slavery and bought by Potiphar who made him steward, a position of trust and responsibility. When Potiphar's wife tried to seduce him, Joseph refused saying, *"Because of me my master has no concern about anything in the house, and he has put everything that he has in my charge. He is not greater in this house than I am, nor has he kept back anything from me except you, because you are his wife. How then can I do this great wickedness and sin against God?"* (Gen. 39:8-9)

As a steward, Joseph the slave felt a keen sense of responsibility because of the great trust that had been placed in him as a servant-steward. Later, Joseph was also given stewardship responsibilities in prison and was ultimately made steward over all of Egypt. (Gen. 41)

The supervision of other people's work is a stewardship responsibility. Paul only used the specific term *oikonomos* once in his letters to Timothy and Titus: *"For an overseer, as God's steward, must be above reproach."* (Titus 1:7) The concept of stewardship as a leadership responsibility, however, is clear in his writings. He referred to his stewardship responsibilities in 1 Timothy 1:4 and in letters to at least three churches. (1 Cor. 9:17; Eph. 3:2; Col. 1:25)

Paul typically is not described as a "Barnabas," which means "son of encouragement" (Acts 4:36), but he certainly seems like one in his writings to these two young leaders whom he encouraged and mentored. He called them both his true sons. He showed personal concern for them, commenting on Timothy's family and his health issues and mentioning to both young leaders that he was sending specific people to help in the work. Paul was transparent with his mentees, sharing with them from his personal experiences, including his struggles, challenges and disappointments, as well as his joys and accomplishments and his desire for them to be near him. (2 Tim. 1:15-17; 2 Tim. 3:10-11; 2 Tim. 4:9; Titus 3:12)

Servant-Stewardship is Still Relevant

By the time the group had completed the exegetical study of the Pastoral Letters, we had an initial list of 77 principles and characteristics. Several similar statements, however, appear more than once in the three letters. In its present form, the list has been combined under 13 broad statements with sub-points that can be useful both in the selection and evaluation of servant-stewards as supervisors. These descriptions of the core character and characteristics of a *servant-steward* apply to anyone who is given a leadership responsibility at any level in any organization.

Leading by Serving

"Whoever would be great among you must be your servant."
(Matthew 20:26)

"Your attitude should be the same as that of Christ Jesus: Who, being in very nature God, did not consider equality with God something to be grasped, but made himself nothing, taking the very nature of a servant..."
(Philippians 2:5-7, NIV)

Servant-stewards demonstrate the power of the presence of the Spirit in their demeanor, not "lording it over others."

- Servant-stewards demonstrate a genuine love for the people they lead. (1 Tim. 1:5-7)
- Servant-stewards see their role of authority as a responsibility, not as a privilege. (1 Tim. 2:2)
- Servant-stewards do not bully the people they lead. (1 Tim. 4:2-3)
- Servant-stewards take seriously their responsibility to live a life of dignity, treating others with proper respect. (1 Tim. 2:2)
- Servant-stewards show genuine concern for the people they lead and provide appropriate help for them to flourish. (1 Tim. 5:1-16)
- Servant-stewards build genuine, caring relationships with the people they lead. (2 Tim. 1:4-6)
- Servant-stewards are transparent about their personal lives and vulnerabilities, allowing their followers the opportunity to know them. (2 Tim. 3:10-11)

9

A Biblical Model of Servant-Stewardship

Practical results can come from following a model of leadership that seeks first to serve rather than being served. Servant-stewardship, however, is more than a formula for success—it is the model that Jesus has mandated for all his followers.

Rehoboam Failed to Employ It

The concept of servant-stewardship was recognized as a pattern for success as early as the reign of King David's grandson, Rehoboam. (1 Kings 12:1-16) After Solomon's death, as Rehoboam began his rule over Israel, he was petitioned to lighten the labor and tribute laws that his father had imposed during the building of the temple. His older advisors counseled him, *"If today you will be a servant to these people and serve them and give them a favorable answer, they will always be your servants."* (1 Kings 12:7)

Rehoboam rejected the counsel of the sage advisors, following instead the advice of younger men who told him to make the burdens on the people even greater than his father had done. As a direct result of his failure to follow the model of a servant-steward, Rehoboam lost his rule over the ten tribes that were to form the Northern Kingdom of Israel under Jeroboam's leadership. Rehoboam did not understand the concept of serving as a leader or that being king meant he was responsible to God as a steward of the people of Israel. As a result, the Kingdom that had become victorious under David and glorious under Solomon became a divided Kingdom that was never to have the same status it had enjoyed under its second and third monarchs.

Leaders who are willing to humble themselves and serve their followers will discover, as Rehoboam's older advisers knew, that the followers will reciprocate with their loyalty.

Rehoboam collided head-on with the Biblical truth: *"Pride goes before destruction, a haughty spirit before a fall."* (Prov 16:18) Henry and Richard Blackaby describe pride as one of the most dangerous pitfalls to leaders: "Pride may well be leaders' worst enemy, and it has caused the downfall of many."[1] Pride can be especially dangerous for the spiritual leader: "Spiritual leaders are God's servants, but pride can cause them to act as if God were their servant, obligated to answer their selfish prayers and to bless their grandiose schemes."[2] Pride causes leaders to lose compassion for their followers and see them as an expendable resource to reach the leader's personal goals, rather than the most important resource to be nurtured through the building of relationships.

Jesus Successfully Modeled It

Leadership is defined by Jesus in one word— *servanthood.* (Mt.18:1-4; 19:30; 20: 8, 16, 20-28; Mk.9:35; Jn.13:14-17) Jesus clearly established that his followers were to become servant-steward leaders when He declared *"whoever wants to become great among you must be your servant, and whoever wants to be first must be slave of all. For even the Son of Man did not come to be served, but to serve, and to give his life as a ransom for many."* (Mk. 10:43b-45) He also referred to the need for leaders to exhibit the trait of humility: *"for he who is least among you all – he is the greatest."* (Lk. 9:48)

Jesus demonstrated how seriously He wanted his disciples to follow the model when He took the role of a slave to wash their feet at his last supper with them before the Passover and his crucifixion:

> *"Now that I, your Lord and Teacher, have washed your feet, you also should wash one another's feet. I have set you an example that you should do as I have done for you. I tell you the truth, no servant is greater than his master, nor is a messenger greater than the one who sent him. Now that you know these things, you will be blessed if you do them."* (Lk. 13:14-17)

Jesus' model of leadership with His disciples demonstrated that the effective leader is not so much interested in climbing a corporate ladder as in becoming the step-support for others to grow in spiritual maturity.

It all boils down to having the same attitude that Jesus had. Though he had positional rights in the eternal universal organization, he humbled himself and took a lower position as a servant in obedience to the Father's plan, so that the ultimate purpose he desired to see fulfilled would be achieved by his followers, even after his death. (Phi. 2:5-11) Jesus could do the things he did because he knew Who he was and Whose he was. He always demonstrated his desire to do the Father's will and not his own. His actions were not always popular or within the accepted practices and regulations of the authorities, but he acted based on what he knew was right in God's eyes. He never lost sight of his purpose in coming to earth—to preach the good news of the kingdom. And he showed us the way to the top by such actions as wrapping a towel around his waist, washing his followers' feet, submitting to a criminal's death on the cross, and leaving the fulfillment of the mission to his followers.

Good supervision is dependent on good leadership, and good leadership cannot be learned from a list of do's and don'ts. It must be learned from the inside out. Following a "how to" list is no substitute for a lifestyle of following the principles found in all of God's Word. Reading devotionals *about* God is no substitute for being devoted *to* God. Developing elaborate and impressive plans that demonstrate our creativity and excellence is no substitute for Kingdom-building plans that originate in the mind of God. Applying all the best practices of leadership is no substitute for applying the *best* practice of servanthood as Jesus demonstrated.

Servant-stewards are persons of integrity, providing a model for others in their teaching and their practice.

- Servant-stewards have no obvious or hidden vices or character flaws. (1 Tim. 4:2-3)
- Servant-stewards are persons of integrity. Their daily lives (public and private) are consistent with their public teaching. (2 Tim. 3:10-11)
- Servant-stewards demonstrate their integrity by practicing at home what they teach in public. (1 Tim. 3:11-12; Titus 1:5-9; Titus 2:7-8)
- Servant-stewards are consistent in the message they communicate. (2 Tim. 1:13; 2:2; 3:10-11)
- Servant-stewards constantly put forth a godly standard for others to follow. (1 Tim. 4:1-5)
- Servant-stewards hold themselves to a high standard of conduct, regardless of their title or position, taking every precaution to avoid even the appearance of evil. (2 Tim. 3:1-9; Titus 1:5; 1 Tim. 1:18; 3:10)
- Servant-stewards lead out of *character* and not out of preferential relationships. (1 Tim. 5:21)

Practical Applications for Today

The Need for Integrity and Credibility in the Leader's Life

Integrity is an essential attribute of character in the life of the leader. Integrity and credibility go hand-in hand—you can't have one without the other. The Blackabys say, "When leaders have integrity, their followers always know what to expect."³ James Kouzes and Barry Posner also found that people want leaders who are credible: "Credibility is the foundation of leadership...on which leaders and constituents build the grand dreams of the future."⁴ Conversely, the loss of integrity and credibility can bring those grand dreams crashing to the ground.

Rehoboam's loss of a united kingdom had been foretold during his father Solomon's reign. Having asked God to grant him wisdom (1 Kings 3:7-9), Solomon was instructed to be a man of integrity as his father David had been. (1 Kings 3:14; 9:4) If Solomon would be a man of integrity, his royal line would last forever:

> *"As for you, if you walk before me in integrity of heart and uprightness, as David your father did, and do all I command and observe my decrees and laws, I will establish your royal throne over Israel forever, as I promised David your father when I said, `You shall never fail to have a man on the throne of Israel.'"* (1 Kings 9:4-5) However, if Solomon or his sons turned to other gods, the Lord God assured him, *"then I will cut off Israel from the land I have given them and will reject this temple I have consecrated for my Name. Israel will then become a byword and an object of ridicule among all peoples."*
> (1 Kings 9:7)

Solomon went on to take 700 wives of royalty and 300 concubines from the peoples with whom God had clearly commanded that the Israelites were not to intermarry. In his later years, Solomon practiced the worship of the goddess Ashtoreth and built places of worship for his wives to practice their foreign religions. Solomon's sexual sin exemplifies one of the most insidious traps that has kept many leaders from finishing well.⁵ Because of this infidelity and his failure to keep the Lord's command, he was told by God that his kingdom would be divided and the son who would succeed him would be left with only one tribe.

(1 Kings 11:1-13) This prophecy was then fulfilled as Rehoboam came into power following Solomon's death. Solomon's lack of integrity led the way to the destruction of his kingdom.

Credibility is an extension of one's trustworthiness. If the leader is found to be untrustworthy in one area of their life, then followers can justifiably question the leader's trustworthiness in all areas of their life.

The most effective leaders recognize their need for accountability partners to help them guard against the danger of thinking that they are immune to the devastation of moral failure. The degree of your effectiveness as a leader in business or in ministry is directly related to the degree to which you demonstrate integrity and credibility in your personal life. You must not just "talk the talk," you have to "walk the walk" and practice what you preach. That means being recognized as a promise-keeper, a man or woman of your word.

The Need for Empowerment to Multiply the Leader's Effectiveness

Empowered people feel that they are valued as people, that what they have to say is also of value, and that they have influence. The word "empowerment" is often confused with delegation of authority. People do not necessarily have to be given a delegated authority, however, to feel empowered. (More on this in the chapter on Teaming for Unity.)

Empowerment requires risk on the part of the leader. Only a secure leader can give empowerment to others. Barriers to empowerment include the desire for job security, resistance to change, and lack of self-worth. By contrast, secure leaders give themselves away as they empower others.

Something as simple as giving credit where credit is due can be empowering. Mark Twain said that great things can happen when you don't care who gets the credit. John Maxwell suggests taking that a step farther: "I believe the

16

greatest things happen *only* when you give others the credit."[6] Ultimately, we should be concerned that God receives the glory rather than who receives the credit. (1 Cor. 10:31)

Most of us probably see leadership as a quality to be found in a few strong people that we call "leaders." Paul Ford challenges that view stating, "Leadership in the body of Christ is a series of functions to be fulfilled by a group of people. Yes, there are still individual leaders or elders to whom we must submit, but the functions of leadership are to be shared."[7]

Can this model be effective in a business setting? We believe it can. Presidents Harry Truman and Ronald Reagan agreed. Both are said to have kept that quote from Mark Twain on their desks! President Abraham Lincoln was famous for deferring and referring decisions to his cabinet members. Shared leadership and empowerment are not new concepts. They have been effectively employed by successful leaders for a very long time.

Servant-stewards prepare for succession.
- Servant-stewards are careful in the selection and endorsement of new leaders. (1 Tim. 5:22)
- Servant-stewards are good judges of character. (1 Tim. 3:12)
- Servant-stewards gather the right people to join them in the task. (2 Tim. 2:1-2; 2 Tim. 4:9-18)

The Need to Reproduce Leaders

Reproduction is closely associated with empowerment. The most effective leaders see great value in investing in others. In most cases, they also were mentored by someone who saw potential in them. As leaders give of themselves to serve those who follow, they can multiply themselves exponentially through the leaders that will emerge.

Some leaders do not empower and reproduce themselves effectively due to their self-imposed pressures of time and perfectionism. Insecure leaders will find it difficult to reproduce themselves, but leaders who share their leadership and train leaders to follow them give power to others and can see explosive growth.

The Need for Margin in the Leader's Life

The speed of change over the last century has continued to gain momentum creating unprecedented levels of stress that can lead to psychological, physiological, and behavioral disorders. Dr. Richard Swenson described this as "overload syndrome." Swenson, a medical doctor, diagnosed the source of this stress as our living in an age that has lost control of progress and is now controlled *by* progress. The object is not to fight progress, but to regain control of it to make it work again for us. The solution, according to Swenson, is in finding and maintaining margin in one's life.[8]

Overload syndrome occurs "whenever the requirements upon us exceed that which we are able to bear."[9] He illustrates by pointing out that a camel's back is not broken by the proverbial straw. The camel is able to bear a very heavy load, but when the maximum weight the camel can carry is reached, one more straw will break its back. In reality, it is not the straw, but the overload that breaks the camel's back. You might be experiencing overload of:

- activity
- change
- choice
- commitment
- debt
- decisions
- education
- expectations
- fatigue

- hurry
- information
- media
- people
- possessions
- technology
- traffic
- work

...even ministry

Overload occurs when our load is greater than our power. Margin, the prescription for overload, is when our power is greater than our load. Swenson puts this in the form of a simple mathematical equation:

Power – Load = Margin

Effective leadership requires a balance in the life of the leader that provides margin in the areas of emotional energy, physical energy, time, and finances.[10] Swenson points out, "Actually, having margin is not a spiritual necessity. But availability is. God expects us to be available for the needs of others."[11] Time management is a key to building margin and the management of time must be based on one's priority relationships. Swenson asserts that establishing priorities will not help one achieve margin if the prioritization is in a sequential order. Instead, he suggests placing God at the center of everything, then building outward from that point.[12] Giving appropriate time to priority relationships, starting with your personal relationship to God, becomes the key to finding margin.

Leadership should be synonymous with servanthood. To effectively serve your followers, you must build a degree of margin in your life that will allow time for teaching them to be less dependent on you as they mature to become leaders of still others. As you lead by serving your followers, this in turn will help to build a relationship of trust, credibility, and mutual accountability.

The Need to Establish Priorities

"Busyness" does not necessarily translate into accomplishment. In a practical sense, the most useful word in your servanthood vocabulary might be the word "no." Only by saying "no" to some activities that are lower priorities can you give the priority time to the relationships that are of higher priority. It is easier to say "no" if you have firmly established your priorities ahead of time. By making the stewardship of your relationships a priority in your own life, you will point others to effectiveness in their work and ministry. As you steward your relationships with the people you lead, you will also set an example for them to be good stewards of their own relationships.

To effectively steward your relationships with the people you are tasked to serve, you must consciously establish priorities for how you will spend your limited time and energy. If you are having trouble prioritizing, try asking this series of questions for each activity that takes up your time:

1. Is this really necessary?
    a. If no, can you eliminate it altogether?
    b. Sometimes there are things you want to do even if they are not really necessary. These can be time wasters, so consider carefully how much time you spend on them.
2. Is this something that you should do personally, or can you delegate it to someone else? Consider the fact that your job as a servant-steward is to equip and release the people you lead—even if you *could* do it better yourself.
    a. If someone else can do it, let them—even if they can only do it 80% as well as you would.[13] This can free you up to work on other priorities and develop more relationships.
    b. What if they can only do it 60% as well as you would for now? Might they learn to do it better by starting now?

   c. If there is no one who can do it now, find someone to train!
3. Is this something that plays to your strength? If so, then you will see the greatest return on your investment of time and energy.
4. Is this something that motivates you? If you are spending too much time and energy on activities that drain you, you will be headed down the path of burnout.

Decision Tree for Prioritizing Your Tasks and Time

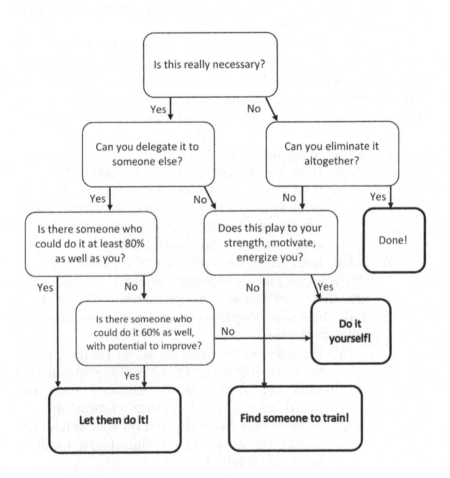

Throughout his ministry, the Apostle Paul demonstrated his priority for knowing Christ and making him known to others. Paul began his personal relationship with Christ asking the question *"Who are you, Lord?"* (Acts 9:5) Years later, toward the end of his career, he was still wanting to grow in his relationship with Christ: *"I want to know Christ..."* (Philippians 3:10a)

Not only did Paul want to know more about the Savior he served, he also wanted his followers to know more about Christ as well:

> *"I keep asking that the God of our Lord Jesus Christ, the glorious Father, may give you the Spirit of wisdom and revelation, so that you may know him better."* (Ephesians 1:17)

> *"My purpose is that they may be encouraged in heart and united in love, so that they may have the full riches of complete understanding, in order that they may know the mystery of God, namely, Christ, in whom are hidden all the treasures of wisdom and knowledge."* (Colossians 2:2-3)

Paul wanted his immediate followers to know Christ and he also established a priority for his followers to carry on, teaching still others what they had learned from him: *"The things you have heard me say in the presence of many witnesses entrust to reliable men who will also be qualified to teach others."* (2 Tim. 2:2) Paul expected his followers to pay it forward, freely giving as they had freely received.

To know Christ and to be like him you must learn to be a servant. The key to effective leadership is found, as Jesus taught his disciples, in serving others, helping them to become all God wants them to be in Him so that He can accomplish all He wants to do through them. In other words, to be the effective leader you are meant to be, you need to be a good steward of the people you have been given to lead. And that is why we call it being a *servant-steward*.

Leadership Hints

1. Take some personal time to make of list of your top priorities in life. Consider all your relationships including family, work, friends—and don't forget your relationship to God.

2. To say "yes" to these priorities, what are some things to which you need to say "no?"

3. Do you have any succession plans for when you will no longer be in your current position? Who could take some of the load off right now? Who are you mentoring?

4. You can serve the people without letting them "run you over." How do you think your supervisees and co-workers would rate you as a servant-steward? What can you do to improve that score?[14]

Supervising for Success

"If he works for you, you work for him."
(Japanese proverb)

Servant-stewards give honor and recognition for the good work of those they lead.

- Servant-stewards communicate clear expectations, then offer help to meet these. (Titus 3:8-9)
- Servant-stewards want their people to succeed. (Titus 3:8-9)
- Servant-stewards validate the gift in others. (1 Tim. 4:14)
- Servant-stewards affirm the faith of others and the power of the Holy Spirit at work in them. (2 Tim. 1:4-6; 1 Tim. 5:17-18)
- Servant-stewards encourage others to work from their giftedness with confidence. (2 Tim. 1:4-6)
- Servant-stewards actively seek feedback from appropriate sources to evaluate the work of their direct reports, adding this to their own observations. (1 Tim. 5:19-24)
- Servant-stewards make it easy for others to give honest feedback. (1 Tim. 5:19-24)
- Servant-stewards strive to be impartial as they make every effort to deal with people equitably. (1 Tim. 5:21)
- Servant-stewards stay in touch with the needs of their followers and are ready to suggest helpful resources when appropriate. (Titus 3:13-14)

What *is* Supervision?

What's the first thought that comes to your mind when you hear the word "supervision"? An administrative chore? Boss? Controlling? Time consuming? Roadblock? Sadly, most people tend to see supervision as a necessary evil that must be endured.

Good supervision, however, can be the secret ingredient that makes an organization great. Supervision can strengthen the life of new personnel through the attention and support you provide. With appropriate supervision, the personnel you supervise become extensions of your work as you share your goals with them. Good supervision can be the most important key to building good morale. The result is increased effectiveness and higher productivity from individuals and teams that contribute to the organization's success in realizing its mission.

Conversely, bad supervision can be *the* major obstacle that keeps an organization from reaching its potential success. When personnel feel undervalued, mistrusted, and treated as objects rather than persons of indispensable worth, morale declines and carries productivity down with it. (More about this later in the chapters on "Teaming for Unity" and "Aligning for Advancement.")

Supervision = *super + vision*. *Super* means over, above, or from a higher perspective. *Vision* means sight. Supervision has to do with overseeing the work of others. In any organization, everyone is under the authority of someone else to some degree. Even CEOs of the largest corporations answer to a board of directors that oversee their work. So, your real work as a supervisor is to be a good *steward* of the personnel you have been given to lead.

It is true that people don't leave jobs or organizations, they leave managers.[15] The reason they leave those managers is because of poor supervision. Workers who do not feel the support of their supervisor will fail to achieve their full potential. They become frustrated and eventually burned out resulting in unfulfilled goals for everyone. Some people have a natural ability for getting people to do their best work. Others have to work harder at it, but the skills of good supervision can be learned.

The Art and Science of Supervision

Supervision, like music, can be seen as both an art and a science. The art of music represents the natural gifts a person possesses. The science of music refers to the music structure and the laborious hours of practice required. "Playing by ear" might be an example of the art of music. Our oldest grandson has an amazing ability to sit at the piano and reconstruct a musical piece he has heard with near perfect rhythm, harmony, and chord structure—and he has never had a piano lesson in his life! On the other hand, he has taken guitar lessons to learn the technique and structures of music theory and classical guitar.

Some people have a natural ability and are especially adept at building relationships and understanding human behavior without specialized supervisory training. In the same way a pianist can "play by ear," their sensitivity enables them to discover and deal with issues naturally.

Your perceptions, however, are not always accurate. The science of supervision can offer a way to check these perceptions and help make the best decisions possible in any given circumstance. Even a "natural" supervisor who is "good with people" or one with years of experience can improve their skills by using good techniques of supervision. A medical doctor may have the uncanny ability to diagnose a condition, but no one would want a surgeon to operate until they had made the necessary tests to confirm their hypotheses. Similarly, the science of supervision offers supervisors training to improve their ability to diagnose issues and assist supervisees in dealing with the issues. Good supervision training can help sharpen your abilities in the art of supervision while also placing at your disposal the tools of the science of supervision. The result can be both a good diagnosis of the problem and a good resolution that leads to team unity and increased productivity.

It's All About Relationships

Is your main focus on the task to be accomplished or is it on the person you are supervising? If your central focus is on the task, you might not realize how that depersonalizes the personnel and makes them feel like an expendable object rather than a fellow worker. And that will result in decreased productivity because disgruntled workers are not the most productive workers. Yes, there is a very important task to be accomplished, and to do that requires every individual in the organization contributing their part to accomplish it. Your focus as a supervisor, however, is not on the task, but on the person. You are not supervising *tasks*, you are supervising *people*. Your work is helping the people you supervise fulfill the task to which they have been assigned. Together, the team can then become highly productive for the organization as each individual does their part.

The most important resource of any organization is its personnel. Even a "fully automated" manufacturing plant requires at least a minimal number of human technicians to maintain it. If anyone on the team becomes burned out or used up, the whole team suffers and ultimately it is the organization's loss—loss of goals that are not met and loss of trust because of a supervisor's insensitivity to their needs as people. You, as a supervisor, are the front line of your organization's integrity with the personnel you serve.

You can best serve your personnel by providing support that includes both the enrichment of personhood and the performance of tasks. If the emphasis is entirely on the performance of tasks, the supervisee will feel treated as a thing rather than a person. Sooner or later they will lose their motivation and be unable to perform tasks properly. Neither is the enrichment of personhood the only object of supervision. That would be a counseling relationship rather than a supervisory relationship.

Both the development of personhood and the performance of tasks are needed in order to achieve successful supervision. The two feed each other. Fulfilling a task is an important way of growing and is therefore part of the development of personhood. As the person grows and feels good about themself as a person, they will become a better worker, contributing more effectively to the goals and objectives of the organization. A good supervisor helps the supervisee conceptualize the task, plan for action, and execute the plan—and then gives recognition for a job well done.

Regardless of the business you are in, it is all about relationships—relationships upline, down-line and laterally with your coworkers. There are also relationships with constituents, suppliers, clients, customers, and end-users. You have been given a stewardship responsibility to develop all these relationships. As a supervisor and representative of your company or organization, you are a relationship steward. Christian believers are in the relationship business of restoring people to a right relationship with God.

In an effort to be fair as a supervisor, you might try to treat everyone exactly the same. That would work very well if the needs and expectations of every individual were exactly the same. Each member of your team, however, is a unique individual with different needs, experience, perspectives, gifts, talents, strengths, interests, and expectations. To be truly fair to each individual you supervise, you need to develop a relationship to get to know first *who* they are, then *what* they really need to accomplish their assignment, and finally *how* to best meet that need. It takes time, but the time invested will result in increased productivity because people want to be valued for who they are and what they have to contribute to a greater cause. Sure, they might also like a bigger salary, but the salary is really just one measurement of the value of what they bring to the organization. There are quite a few studies available that prove salaries don't actually improve morale at a certain level of employment. Paying people fairly is one thing, but merely increasing salary has not been proven to improve morale or productivity once you get past some fairly entry-level positions.

(See more about this in the chapter on "Aligning for Advancement.")

Adjust Your Style to the Needs of the Person

Supervisors often fall into a comfortable pattern of functioning with a particular model of supervision they have observed elsewhere. A supervisor with military experience might use a command model at the exclusion of all others. Another supervisor might expect his supervisees to figure out on their own how to do the job and basically just manage themselves. The best supervision, however, occurs when the supervisor learns to adjust their style to use the model that best fits the situation. You need to examine each supervisory situation separately to determine the needs of your supervisee and implement the best supervision model needed at the time.

Four basic styles of supervision define the supervisor's relationship to the supervisee as they grow in their development or expertise related to a specific task or assignment: Directing, Mentoring, Coaching and Encouraging. As an individual grows in their expertise, it is your responsibility as a supervisor to adjust your style to match their needs. The supervisee cannot decide arbitrarily to start out in the second, third, or fourth style, nor can they set dates to be at certain levels of development. Together, however, you can determine the level of development for the specific task, and then as the person moves from one state into another, you will know how to adjust your style of supervision. Be aware also that movement from one level to the next is not absolute. After leaving one level, a person may revert back to it from time to time.[16]

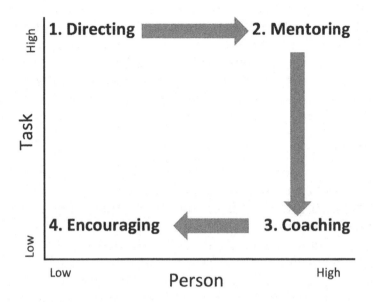

Directing

The first style, Directing, has high focus on task with a low focus on the person. It is the most structured of all the styles. In the beginning, the supervisor must tell the supervisee about the task and outline responsibilities, resources, and methods for doing the work. Although there is a need to build relationship with the supervisee, the supervisor recognizes that the person will become frustrated and begin to feel like a failure if they are not given instruction and guidance to do the task at hand. Focusing on the task at this stage will lay the groundwork for building the relationship.

Mentoring

As the person begins to gain some understanding of the task, you can move to a Mentoring style. A mentor is a source of wisdom, teaching, and support who sometimes offers advice based on their own experience. At this stage of development, the supervisor begins to take the personhood of the supervisee into greater consideration while continuing to place high focus on the task. By this time, the supervisee has learned about the structure and the responsibilities and has demonstrated commitment to the work. You must determine if the supervisee understands their role in accomplishing the organizational objectives and not just the mechanics of the task.

Coaching

Moving from Mentoring to Coaching may be difficult for some supervisors because Coaching is more focused on the person with lower focus on the task. When the supervisee reaches this stage of development, they are capable of making their own plans and evaluating their own effectiveness at the task. At this stage of development, the supervisee has attained to a level of competency but might need some encouragement to follow through with a plan to do what they know how to do.

Be careful, however, not to assume that the relationship can get to this level of development without passing through the first two stages. At the same time, you should not assume that everyone is a rank beginner with every new task. If the supervisee is a veteran worker, they might already have transferrable skills that can help them to go quickly to this level. Either way, the primary focus at this stage is on building relationship with your supervisee and coaching them to achieve their maximum potential. You no longer have to spend time showing them how to do the task.

Encouraging

The Encouraging style requires little energy focused on either personhood or task. By the time the supervisee has reached this stage of development, they should be "low maintenance." There is increased respect for and trust of the person when they grow to only need encouragement. At this point, trust translates into increased responsibility for the supervisee. You begin to see the supervisee as a partner in the assignment who has a voice in decisions and greater ownership of plans and actions.

Sometimes supervisors fear moving into the Encouraging phase because they must give away some control. At this stage, if the supervisee feels you are looking over their shoulder, they may feel disempowered or that you lack trust in their ability to do their job. This lack of trust becomes a roadblock, not only to the development of the supervisee, but also to the growth of the organization. (See more about this in the chapter on "Teaming for Unity.")

The supervisee at this stage is now capable of leading, mentoring, or coaching others, as they have mastered the task or skill and are gaining both self-confidence and the confidence of their supervisor. Supervision of a worker at this stage mainly involves periodic check-ins for encouragement and verification that the supervisee has all the necessary tools to do the job.

Be careful, however, not to allow the relationship to be taken for granted. Although there is a low focus on relationship building at this stage, you still need to give some attention to maintaining the relationship. Low focus does not mean no focus.

Using the Different Styles to Supervise

Growing through the stages and adapting your style to each is very much like parenting. In fact, you pass through these same stages of development as you help your child grow from total dependency as an infant, to independency as an adolescent, to interdependency as an adult. When a new person arrives on the job, begin with the highest structure you will ever need using a directive style. This is an opportunity to help the new coworker define roles and responsibilities. It is just as unrealistic to expect the new worker to begin in any other stage as it would be to expect an infant to begin life with the expectations you would have for an adolescent or adult. Be careful, however, not to treat your new personnel as children! We are only talking about providing structure for them to learn and adjust to their new assigned roles and assignments. Don't assume that they know all the written or unwritten expectations that come with the job. They will need orientation to the culture of the company.

The biggest challenge can be when you have several supervisees at different levels of development in their assignments. Because of different levels of maturity, training, experience, and previous relationships, each individual will move through each of the stages at varying paces. New supervisees will take more time to advance through the stages than supervisees with tenure. And some people will take longer at the later stages, even after moving quickly through the earlier ones. As a supervisor, you need to know each of your supervisees well enough to keep up with their individual levels of development and supervisory needs. A person in an early stage of supervision who does not understand the dynamics of the different styles may think the supervisor is playing favorites or may feel inadequate.

As a new regional leader in western South America,[17] I asked three men to join my leadership team. The first two, Tom and Brian, I had known for several years, and I was inviting them to fill roles they had already been filling with years of experience. Steve, however, was new to the role he would be filling. After a few weeks on the job, Steve came into my office in an obvious state of agitation. Why, he asked, was I spending so much time looking over his shoulder and shadowing him on the job when it was obvious that I was not doing the same with Tom or Brian? He felt I did not trust him the way I trusted his other teammates.

I explained that Tom was in almost exactly the same position he had been filling previously, so he knew his job better than I did. Brian and I had worked closely together in similar roles before, so I knew that he knew where I was headed and where I felt we needed to go as a region. I did not have to spend much time directing either of them to be sure we were all saying the same thing and rowing together as a team. Steve, however, was new to the role and, although he had previous leadership experience, had never been in any leadership responsibility in the organization. I had first met him when I invited him to be interviewed for the position, so we had no previous relationship. I assured him that the role he was filling was so important to help us get to where we needed to go that I had to be absolutely certain that he and I were on the same page and had the same understanding of where we were going and how we would get there. Little by little and very soon, I promised, as we grew to know each other better and gained confidence in each other, we would be going in our own independent directions, multiplying our leadership throughout the region. That is exactly what happened within a few short months and for the next seven years we worked together as a highly productive and effective team.

Clarify Expectations

Clarifying expectations early on can help reduce potential frustrations between you and your supervisee. I should have explained my reasoning to Steve from the beginning of our relationship to avoid making him feel that I did not have confidence in him.

A problem may develop when people have an idealized concept of supervision. Young people who are just entering the workforce might see supervision as what they experienced in their families or in the classroom. Even experienced workers can have expectations from their previous employment. They may idealize the supervisory relationship as being egalitarian on one extreme or autocratic on the other. The supervisory relationship cannot be egalitarian because the supervisor is always held accountable for the supervisee and must, in turn, hold the supervisee accountable. At the same time, it should not become autocratic.

When a friend becomes your assigned supervisee, you can still have a close personal relationship, but you should define your supervisory relationship carefully. It should be clear to others that you are not showing favoritism in the way you supervise the friend. Neither should you treat your friend in such a way as to penalize them in your effort to not show them favoritism.

Use Assessments to Adjust Your Style to Needs

In addition to adjusting your style to the developmental needs of the individual with regard to the assigned task, you should also adjust the way you relate to the individual according to their personality. Spiritual gifts should also be taken into consideration in the case of a Christian co-worker. The right assessments administered at the right time in the right way with the help of the right consultant or coach can help you better understand the kind of environment each supervisee needs to "fit and flourish" in their assignment.

Keep in mind, though, that assessments are only tools. No assessment can magically transform a poor performer into a highly productive team member. If, however, you know how to use the results of the assessment over a period of time, the assessment can give valuable insights that can lead to significant change for healthier, more productive individuals and teams. In the chapter on "Teaming for Unity," we will talk more about using assessments as an aid to build unity in the team.

Of the many assessments we have tried, we have found The Birkman Method® and *Your Leadership Grip* to be the most effective to facilitate personal development, develop leadership skills, and improve communication between supervisors and the people they supervise.

The Birkman Method® has many unique components and is much more than just a personality assessment. It identifies not only your Usual style of behavior (when you are most effective), but also your Stress behavior (your less effective or "frustrated" style). Most importantly and uniquely, Birkman explains *why* you sometimes might behave one way and other times in another way. Birkman highlights the fact that 70% of the time, the way we act is *not* how we want to be treated by others. The assessment helps you understand what you need from coworkers to stay productive and less stressed and also how you can support them to be their best.[18]

Grip-Birkman, for faith-based groups, combines The Birkman Method® with *Your Leadership Grip*, a spiritual gifts assessment that guides individuals to discover their gifts combination in the context of "body life."[19] *Your Leadership Grip* takes a unique approach to gifts assessment by examining your spiritual gifts through three different lenses. First, you determine your specific gift combination, focusing on the top four gifts. Then you look at your preferred "Team Styles"—how you use your gifts as you fulfill your part in the group setting. Next, you examine your "Body Building Roles"—the roles you play in helping the team fulfill its mission. Specific Team Styles and Body Building Roles match with specific gifts and gift combinations.

By examining your gifts through the three lenses as corners of a triangle, Your Leadership Grip helps guide you to confirm and affirm the presence of your gift combination through a process of "confirming the integrity" of the three corners. There is also an opportunity to use a 360-degree questionnaire to gain input and the insights of close friends or coworkers who have seen you engaging your gifts in ministry.

Looking at personality alone will not provide a complete picture of how or why you behave the way you do in any given situation. Grip-Birkman provides an opportunity to see how you are sometimes able to operate quite effectively outside the natural comfort zones of your personality because of the supernatural work of the Spirit in you.

The Birkman and Grip-Birkman provide a common language to begin a dialogue that can lead to more effective communication. These assessments can help you grow in both your self-awareness and your social awareness as you discover how your perspective affects your expectations and how these influence your behavior.

Using information from Grip-Birkman or The Birkman Method in the supervisory relationship, you can gain invaluable insights into how the individual prefers to be treated. Birkman calls this Needs or expectations. You can learn how to use this information to help them to be at their best, most positive, and effective self (Usual Style of behavior) and to help them avoid their less effective, less positive behaviors (Stress Style) that result when their Needs or expectations are not being met.

Have Them Write Their Personal User Manual

After the individual has gained some understanding of their strengths, needs, and how they view themselves and others, have them write their own "Personal User Manual." (A copy of the form is in the Appendix.) This is where they can summarize some of the insights they have gained from their assessments. Assure them that this is not a graded paper. The purpose is to help you do a better job of supervising them to be their very best—to flourish in their job.

You can use the suggestions from their Personal User Manual to help you personalize the way you relate to each person you supervise. For example, one person might want you to be very direct in the way you tell them what you want from them, while another person might prefer you use more passive language to offer suggestions and then allow them to act with a little more liberty. Some people will want more group interaction and others will prefer to work alone.

You should also share your own Personal User Manual with the people you supervise. Your vulnerability and transparency will encourage them to be open and honest about what they need to be effective in their work. It will also serve to help them understand what you want and expect from them to help you be the best supervisor you can be.

Servant-stewards focus on positive goals.

• Servant-stewards demonstrate a positive attitude, focusing on what God is providing, rather than on what is not available. (1 Tim. 1:8-10, 16-17)

• Servant-stewards are more concerned with godly living than with worldly gain. (1 Tim. 6:3-10)

• Servant-stewards possess an inner strength of contentment with what God has provided them. (1 Tim. 6:3-10)

• Servant-stewards communicate clear expectations, then offer help to meet these. (Titus 3:8-9)

Covenant Together

Covenants are necessary for good supervision. Covenants are not job descriptions, although the two must be compatible. The comparison chart below shows the difference between the two.

Job description	Covenant
• Relates to task issues • Generic list of responsibilities that apply to anyone who accepts the job • Developed by the employing agency • Contains more duties than a person can work on at any one time	• Relates to task and personhood issues • Personal, relates to a specific person who has a responsibility • Negotiated together by the supervisor and supervisee • Helps define the specific responsibilities and priorities from the job description that the individual will work on during a specific period of time.

Apart from the formal covenant, be careful to avoid adding informal or tacit expectations. These unwritten expectations are driven by a spoken or unspoken rule ("We have this formal covenant, but what we will really do is....") and are subject to game-playing disclaimers such as "I didn't say that" or qualifications such as "But that is not what I meant." Adding such expectations outside the written covenant can undermine the success of your supervisee, create suspicion, confuse accountability, and can quickly erode trust. Just don't do it!

The Covenant Process

Four areas should be covered in a covenant—needs, goals, activities and evaluation. Your organization might use its own special terms to describe these areas, but the process is the same.

1. Determine the Need

First, determine what is the need to be addressed. The rest of the process will flow out of this need. The need serves as the overall "big picture" for the work. The need should reflect something that, if met, will help the individual, team, and organization to be more productive toward fulfilling the organization's mission.

2. Set SMS Goals

Goals provide one of the most important parts of the covenant. They serve as a road map for relating to others, especially the supervisor. Some organizations promote the writing of "*SMART*" goals. We have found that many people have trouble remembering what the five letters in the SMART acrostic stand for, so we have been using *SMS* to write goals. A good goal will be *Specific, Measurable,* and *Strategic.*[20]

While the need is general, goals should be *specific,* showing how they will address the need. The goal needs to be specific enough that you can tell when and how well it has been accomplished.

Goals should be *measurable,* so you will know when the goal has been met. Goals should also be attainable. It is tempting to set goals that are idealistic and unreasonable given the time, situation, and resources. (This is not to say we should not pray to God to do immeasurably beyond what we can ask or imagine. Eph. 3:20)

Strategic refers to the need for the goal to be "nested" in the goals of the team, the supervisor, and the goals of the organization. A good goal can easily be identified as contributing in some way to the purpose for which the organization exists. Even personal development goals can be for the benefit of the organization because a healthier worker will be a more productive worker. If the goal is addressing a need that will benefit the organization, then it will be *strategic.*

It is always best for goals to be written "top down" in the organization. Leaders at every level should write their own goals to address needs that reflect the needs and goals of the organization. They should then share these with the personnel they supervise. This will provide both a model for personnel at the next level to follow while also helping to make sure their goals are compatible with and contributing to the goals of their leaders and the organization.

It is also good to include personal development goals as well as work goals. Personal development goals may deal with relationships or areas of the individual's personal growth. Review the goals carefully to ensure they are reasonable. The supervisee must not be caught between conflicting goals set by the organization and the supervisor.

Goals are not static and may need to be revised. The covenant should be dated, and a review time should be designated for revising the goals when new situations arise or self-awareness increases.

3. Plan Appropriate Activities

Each goal will need multiple activities or action plans designed to reach the specific goal. This is where you will outline the responsibilities and roles for accomplishing the stated goal. At this point you should also be able to determine what style of supervision is needed for the specific tasks your supervisee will be addressing. As you examine the supervisee's level of skill and confidence related to the specific task, together you can determine if they need more direction, mentoring, coaching, or just encouragement to "go for it!"

4. Evaluate the Results

Each goal requires an evaluation process that includes a date set to accomplish the goal. The criteria for evaluation are as necessary as the process. How will you know they did what they set out to do? A well-written goal will have a timeframe written in, so evaluation should be relatively easy. All too often, however, the evaluation phase is neglected, passing up a golden opportunity to affirm, praise, encourage, and prepare personnel for growing as they repeat the cycle of addressing new needs and writing new goals.

The process does not need to be painful. After a few cycles, your personnel should begin to see that you are not using their goals as a stick to beat them over the head or as a carrot to coerce them into complying with meaningless company policy, but rather as a means to help them to be more successful in their assignment. That's good for everyone, right?

Clarify Expectations in the Covenant

What percentage of the personnel's work time should each task or goal require? You and your supervisee might have different ideas about which are most important or how much time will be required to complete each task or goal. The wise supervisor will be concerned about not only the task time, but also the supervisee's time for study, family, and spiritual renewal. Make sure your supervisees are not putting unrealistic expectations on themselves that will require taking work over into personal or family time.

At the same time, be clear on any expectations that you or the organization might require. If there are any corrective actions that have been taken, be sure these are also reflected in the goals of the covenant in response to the corrective action. (For more on corrective actions, see the chapter on "Confronting for Change.")

Renegotiation

Changes in circumstances and relationships may require the covenant to be re-evaluated and rewritten. If you are having periodic supervisory meetings, the opportunity to renegotiate a goal can surface. This gives the covenant a chance to work and prevents change on a whim. Renegotiation, as part of the original covenant, is done by mutual consent of the supervisor and the supervisee.

Preparing the Covenant

As you elaborate any form, remember to KISS it:
Keep
It
Short and
Simple.

(Yes, we know. We also first heard of KISS as Keep It Short, Stupid, but we really did not want to offend you with that!)

The covenant really does not need to be very long. Keeping it short and simple will make it much more likely to be a practical tool that is not stuffed away in a forgotten folder until the next annual performance review.

Use the *Covenant Worksheet* in the Appendix to help your personnel prepare for the initial dialogue that begins the process toward writing a covenant agreement. These questions must be answered prior to the writing of the covenant. If the supervisee has a good understanding of their assignment, they should be able to answer these questions well enough to complete the form. The first time for new personnel will require more time and patience. Keep in mind that some people have a lower "Literary" interest.[21]

For these people, writing the document will be a greater challenge, not because they are "illiterate," but because they are likely to be more verbal processors or they want to "just do it." You might consider setting up a time to dialogue and get verbal answers to the questions in a natural, conversational interchange. You can then follow up with a summary that could help as they develop and execute their covenant plan.

The next step will be to transfer the information from the worksheet to the pages of the covenant itself. The covenant should not be a very long document, preferably not more than one or two pages. If your organization does not already have a specific form to follow, adapt the sample form included in the Appendix. You might prefer to use a spreadsheet program to keep each personnel's form available electronically whenever you are traveling.

Dialoguing for Development
Providing feedback in
supervisory/performance conversations

People understand each other by talking.[22]
(Spanish maxim)

*"Think over what I say, for the Lord will give you
understanding in everything."*
(2 Tim. 2:7)

> **Servant-stewards recognize their need for
> the grace of God as the basis for their success.**
> - Servant-stewards recognize their own need
>   for grace and extend grace to others as they
>   exercise their responsibilities.
>   (Titus 3:15; 1 Tim. 1:12-17)
> - Servant-stewards coach, give advice or
>   counsel, and then allow the Lord to do the
>   work. (2 Tim. 2:8-9)

Here is a potentially fatal mistake that supervisors in
every business make all too often: They jump through the
company hoops and make sure all their personnel comply by
writing and uploading their goals into the system and then
never look at them again until the next required annual
review period. It's potentially fatal because the personnel are
likely to see the whole process of goal-writing as
perfunctory. Then, in that annual review, when any of the
written goals have not been met, it is too late to do anything
about it. That can be deflating and discouraging for the
supervisee.

If, on the other hand, you keep the goals in active
memory by reviewing them in periodic supervisory meetings
throughout the year, you can use this as an opportunity for

affirmation and encouragement. In your periodic meetings, ask how the person is doing, what progress are they making, what kind of help they might need, whether the goal needs to be adjusted or renegotiated, or how you can assist in any way. All this can communicate that you really want them to succeed in their job. And if they succeed, you succeed and the organization succeeds.

Good supervision includes regular and frequent meetings between the supervisor and supervisee to review their work and to provide development and support. Regularly scheduled supervisory conversations provide a routine that will minimize the anxiety which normally occurs in a supervisory relationship. This is not a staff meeting. It is a one-on-one dialogue where each party helps develop the agenda.

Schedule Weekly, Biweekly or Monthly Dialogues

We suggest an absolute minimum of monthly scheduled meetings. Some personnel will require more frequent meetings, especially as you are getting to know each other in the early stages of development and learning their assignment. You should calendar these meetings well in advance and with the frequency you agree upon.

A. Prepare Before the Conversation

Both supervisor and supervisee should use this outline to prepare for your dialogue.

1. **Review your own and the other individual's personality profile and consider how they prefer to be treated** in the following areas (based on "Needs" from their Birkman or Grip-Birkman Report).
    a. Emotional Energy: do they prefer an unemotional environment, separating emotions from business, or do they feel more comfortable being open and expressing emotions in conversation?

b. Social Energy: do they need more time to work alone, or do they prefer to work in a team setting?

c. Physical Energy: do they need more time to reflect and control their own agenda, or do they prefer a busy schedule?

d. Self-Consciousness: do they need direct and straightforward communication, or do they prefer more diplomacy that shows respect for them as a person (especially from a supervisor)?

e. Assertiveness: do they need a non-directive, democratic style of supervision, or do they need to know clearly who is in charge?

f. Insistence: do they need a more informal and flexible routine, or do they prefer a more structured environment with a definite plan in place?

g. Incentives: do they tend to measure team success as a group, or do they need a means of measuring and rewarding their personal performance?

h. Restlessness: do they need an environment with few distractions to allow them to focus, or do they prefer variety in their work and deal well with interruptions?

i. Thought: Do they make quick decisions, or do they need time to reflect and consider all angles and possible consequences? Do they prefer to have a general outline, or do they need to have a detailed agenda in advance?

2. **Review written notes from previous meeting.** Be prepared to discuss progress on any goals that were set or tasks that were to be followed up.

3. **Set goals and priorities for the meeting.** What do you hope to take away from the meeting?

4. **Develop your agenda.** Prioritize any items you want to be sure are covered in the meeting.

B. The Conversation

1. **Break the ice** - small talk
2. **Negotiate the agen**da - yours and theirs
3. **Review any tasks, goals or assignments from last meeting**
4. **Work through the prioritized agenda**
5. **Set goals or assign tasks to be completed by the next meeting.** If time runs out, what needs to be carried forward?
6. **Calendar time and place of next meeting**

C. After the Conversation

1. **Take notes for future sessions** (independently for both)
2. **Review and document the meeting** (for supervisor)
   a. Facts - observations
   b. Impressions – feelings
   c. Note any future issues needing work

"The Servant-Steward Coaching Guide" included in the Appendix can be used in a weekly, biweekly, or monthly checkup meeting. Two versions are provided—one for business and one for ministry leaders. You might want to give your supervisees a copy of the questions so they can consider how they rate themselves before your dialogue. For more on a coaching approach to supervision, see the chapter that follows, "Coaching for Effectiveness."

Semi-annual and annual reviews

Every six months you should plan to sit down with each supervisee individually to review their progress toward the goals you have agree upon. In the annual review, you should include 360 degree input from teammates and others who are familiar with the individual's work. (A sample 360 Degree Feedback and Evaluation Form is included in the Appendix.) If this person supervises others, feedback from direct reports should be included. As a supervisor, you will want to write up your own evaluation separately. Then, in the evaluation dialogue, you can share the composite feedback from others and provide additional comments or context from your own observations.

In the conversation, be sure to hear first from the individual, then give feedback from others, and finally give your own conclusions. Ask questions to stimulate conversation. Avoid allowing this to become a time when you are doing most of the talking. To begin the dialogue, ask the individual how they feel about the last six months. What have they seen as some of their best progress toward each of their goals? Save the challenges for later. Work together to set development goals based on the feedback and dialogue.

We suggest including the 360 feedback in the annual review and not in the six-month review to keep this from becoming overly burdensome for those providing the feedback. Both you and your supervisee, however, should prepare your own evaluations in both the six-month and the annual reviews. The mid-year review should be a briefer dialogue to discuss progress or signs of improvement from the annual review.

It takes time to think through and write good reviews, but the time invested can be well worth the effort if you are able to help your supervisees set good goals, make appropriate course corrections when needed, and celebrate progress toward accomplishing the goals that you and they have agreed upon.

Coaching for Effectiveness

"You've got to be very careful if you don't know where you are going, because you might not get there."
(Yogi Berra)

"The purposes of a man's heart are deep waters, but a man of understanding draws them out."
(Prov. 20:5)

Servant-stewards are player-coaches.
- Servant-stewards recognize, respect, and submit to the authority of others over them. (1 Tim. 2:2; 1 Tim. 6:1-2; Titus 2:9-10)
- Servant-stewards are willing to "get their hands dirty," sharing in the work with those they lead. (1 Tim. 1:2; 2 Tim. 2:3-13)
- Servant-stewards know they cannot do the job by themselves. They recognize their need for the Holy Spirit and value the help of others. (2 Tim. 2:1- 2)
- Servant-stewards are lifelong learners. They recognize that godliness requires continual training. (1 Tim. 4:10, 16)

Do you prefer the carrot or the stick approach to management? How about a third option? The power of coaching is being recognized by many managers and leaders as a vital addition to their personal effectiveness toolbox. A coaching approach to supervision can help your direct reports find the self-motivation to be peak performers.

Coaching can be an effective way to deliver feedback that motivates and inspires, and ultimately helps create an environment where employees perceive manager guidance as useful and meaningful.

The principles outlined in this chapter provide a summary of how to use a coaching approach to supervision that expands on the concept of an evaluation dialogue. By applying the basic skills of coaching as you dialogue with your supervisees, you can:

- Provide clarity and direction on responsibilities.
- Assist direct reports to set goals they fully own.
- Increase direct reports' motivation.
- Build trust.
- Improve feedback delivery skills.
- Gain confidence in delivering both affirming and constructive feedback.
- Provide tools necessary for success.

Coaching is not the only effective style of supervision. At times there will be a need for a more directive approach. We have found, however, that a coaching approach to supervision can be very effective in a variety of situations. Whenever possible and appropriate, coaching can be a strong tool for building unity and increasing effectiveness. The greatest advantage to using a coaching approach is the focus on motivating the coachee (person being coached) to take ownership of the actions the coachee decides to take.

If you are already familiar with coaching, then these principles will be a simple review of basic coaching skills. If you are new to coaching, we strongly encourage you to consider the possibility of attending a basic coach training or workshop. You will not become a professional coach from one workshop. You can, however, gain new skills that can help you and your supervisee to have more positive and productive conversations.

Definitions

Coaching is different from consulting, advising, mentoring, or counseling, although some elements of each of these might appear in a supervisory dialogue. To distinguish what coaching is and is not, we will define the following:

- *Consulting*: giving advice, making suggestions of what the person should do.
- *Mentoring*: modeling, showing the person how the mentor did it.
- *Counseling*: dealing with something that's wrong, focusing on healing and recovery from past or current issues.
- *Coaching*: focused on the future, helping the person to discover what to do, setting goals and taking action.

A coaching approach can be useful for supervisors, mentors, consultants, or counselors. It offers a viable alternative to the "carrot or stick" approach as it focuses on helping coachees take ownership of their goals and actively develop their roadmap to accomplish these goals. This can become a powerful motivator to increase the entire team's effectiveness.

The Purpose of the Coaching Session

The purpose of the coaching session is to help the coachee determine one or two specific goals that will help them to become more effective in their present job assignment. Remember SMS as you coach the person to write good goals:

Specific goals are concise and should be attainable within a reasonably short time. Most goals in the coaching context should be attainable in one to two weeks. Vague goals are hard to remember and hard to achieve. Don't focus on long range goals. Focus on the next step. The main question is, "What do you think you need to do now?"

Measurable means there is some way to determine when the goal has been met. Ask, "How will you know if you have completed the goal?"

Strategic goals fit into and contribute to the team and organizational goals and objectives. Strategic goals also are in alignment with and reflect the team and organizational values. A good question to ask here might be, "How will this goal help your team to reach the goals of your organization?" or "To which team or organizational goal will this be contributing?"

The Time Frame of the Coaching Session

Most coaching sessions should be between 30 and 60 minutes in length. You need enough time to help the coachee work through the process of determining a good, actionable goal. At the same time, setting a time limit helps to keep the conversation focused on the purpose of the session.

The Coach's Toolkit

Coaching for effectiveness involves finding the right tools or skills and learning to use these appropriately. The most basic and essential tools you need in your toolkit include: active listening, observing, receiving insight from the Holy Spirit, asking powerful questions, encouraging, providing concise messages, and sometimes assessments.

Active Listening

Active listening means being fully engaged and focused on the coachee. Avoid distractions and the temptation to multi-task during a coaching conversation. Although a statement might prompt an idea you feel urged to share, don't interrupt. Make a quick note and share the idea later if it is still relevant. Active listening can also include casual phrases to clarify briefly as needed or to paraphrase and ensure that you are accurately understanding what is being said.

Observing

Pay attention to both the content and the context that surrounds the content of what the coachee is saying. *How* the words are said (including body language and tone of voice) can be as important as the choice of words to express an idea. Pay attention also to what is *not* being said. Unspoken messages can sometimes communicate as much as words that are spoken.

Receiving Insight from the Holy Spirit

Create an environment in which you and the coachee can hear from the Lord. When appropriate, praying before and after the session can make a difference. If the coachee is also a Christian believer, we like to open the session with the coach praying and ask the coachee to lead the closing prayer. Even if the coachee is not a believer, you can privately ask the Lord to give you insight in the session.

Asking Powerful Questions—the most valuable tool of the coach

Coaches know that the most valuable tool in their skill toolkit is the art of asking questions. A common theme in coaching is *"Ask. Don't Assume."* The goal is not to demonstrate your ability to know what the other person is going to say before they say it, but to help the person develop a plan that is theirs from the beginning. To be effective in using a coaching approach to supervision, learn to ask powerful, open-ended (as opposed to "yes or no") questions. Open-ended questions provoke thought and lead to action. By asking questions you can help others to:

- Gain information
- Grow in their personal discovery
- Generate options
- Uncover obstacles
- Determine next steps

Powerful questions encourage the sharing of ideas and information. They are relevant and thought-provoking. They demand a response that will prompt action.

Some people are naturally inquisitive and find it very easy to ask questions. Others sometimes need help asking good questions, especially when the subject is familiar to us and we have a certain level of personal expertise. With practice, however, you will discover how exciting it can be to ask a powerful question (or a series of questions) that evokes not just an answer but leads the coachee to a plan of action that they are fully committed to carrying out on their own.

Powerful questions are open-ended and ask for specific information from the coachee. Jesus was a master at asking powerful questions that demanded a specific response or commitment from the listener. We have provided some examples below of powerful questions and examples of how Jesus used them in his teaching.

What do you want?
> *"What do you want me to do for you?"* (Mt. 20:32)
> *"Do you want to be healed?"* (Lk. 5:6)

What do you need based on what you currently have?
> *"How many loaves do you have?"* he asked. *"Go and see."* When they found out, they said, *"Five— and two fish."* (Mk. 6:38)

What do you think?
> *"... When Peter came into the house, Jesus was the first to speak. "What do you think, Simon?" he asked. "From whom do the kings of the earth collect duty and taxes—from their own sons or from others?"* (Mt. 17:25)

> *"What do you think about the Christ? Whose son is he?"* (Mt. 22:42)

> *"Who do men say that I am?"* (Mt. 16:13; Mk. 8:27; Lk. 9:18)

"Who do you say that I am?" (Mt. 16:15; Mk. 8:29; Lk. 9:19)

What will be the cost or consequence of your action or the situation?
"You don't know what you are asking," Jesus said. "Can you drink the cup I drink or be baptized with the baptism I am baptized with?" (Mk. 10:38)

In what or whom are you putting your trust?
"Therefore I tell you, do not worry about your life, what you will eat or drink; or about your body, what you will wear. Is not life more important than food, and the body more important than clothes? Look at the birds of the air; they do not sow or reap or store away in barns, and yet your heavenly Father feeds them. Are you not much more valuable than they? Who of you by worrying can add a single hour to his life?" (Mt. 6:25-27)

Whom else could you ask or where else might you look for advice or insight?
"Haven't you read what David did when he and his companions were hungry?" (Mt. 12:3)

"What is written in the Law?" he replied. "How do you read it?" (Lk. 10:26)

Encouraging

Encourage the coachee by speaking words of hope, approving the excellent, or pointing out potential. In the supervisory dialogue, words of encouragement can give the coachee a sense of empowerment.

When speaking words of encouragement, be careful to use the word "and" more than "but." Everything in the phrase preceding the conjunction is negated by the word "but." Be careful also to avoid using the word "encourage" when you really mean "challenge." If your intent is to challenge the coachee to do something or to reconsider something they have said, then say so using clear, direct language.

Providing Concise Messages

Concise messages of seven to ten words of relevance can also be a powerful tool...when used judiciously! We tend to remember concise messages. We do not remember paragraphs so easily. A concise message can help the coachee to *hear* what they are saying or to refocus the train of thought in a direction he had not considered before. Keep your personal suggestions to a minimum. The concise message might begin with:

- "I hear you saying..."
- "You said..."
- "Have you considered..."
- "Here's a resource that might be helpful..."
- "So, your goal is to..."

If the coachee seems to be contradicting themself, to keep from sounding judgmental you might say, "I see this. I hear this. Help me to understand, because it seems to me that they don't match." Then let the coachee respond.

Assessments

Sometimes you need a special tool for a particular job. Adding assessments to your toolkit can help your coachee gain valuable additional insights as they focus on their plan of action. If you are qualified to use any assessments that require certification, by all means use them. You can also call on another coach or consultant to administer an assessment and help with the interpretation of results.

Assessments can often be helpful in such areas as: personality, strengths, career exploration, conflict styles, emotional intelligence, professional interests, and interpersonal relationships.[23] Other assessments might be helpful for guiding the coachee to write their personal mission, vision, and values statements.[24] For Christian believers, a spiritual gifts assessment can be helpful.[25]

Challenges for the Coaching Supervisor

As a supervisor, consider which of the common mistakes listed below is hardest for you and then work to overcome the challenge these present.

1) *Talking too much.* Coaching is about allowing the coachee to speak and discover answers for themselves. If you find yourself talking about yourself, your experiences, or your expertise and not allowing the coachee to speak, you may be talking too much. Master coach Jane Creswell suggested the acrostic, **WAIT**, is good to keep in mind while coaching. Ask yourself:
   Why
   Am
   I
   Talking?

   If we were to observe your coaching sessions from across the room without being able to hear the conversation, we should be able to tell who is the coachee by who is talking the most.

2) *Problem solving for the other person.* Coaching is about drawing answers from the other person so they can solve the problems, not solving the problems for them.

3) *Not staying in your role as coach.* It is easy to revert to counseling, consulting, or directing. Although you, as a supervisor, will sometimes need to be directive, be careful to do so only when necessary. Make it clear that you are being directive on this specific issue at this specific time for these reasons. If you fall into directive

mode too often, you will lose the effectiveness of a coaching approach to supervision.

4) *Letting your own buttons be pushed.* Although you might feel passionate about the issues that come up in the conversation, keep the session focused on the coachee and the issues they want to address.

5) *Getting caught up in the coachee's drama.* Remain focused on guiding the coachee toward goals and don't be distracted by personal issues that should be addressed by a counselor. Many counselors will also use a coaching approach to help their clients toward healing, but that is not your purpose here. If it looks like the person needs to be referred to a counselor or an experienced life coach, then make the referral.

6) *Not getting clear agreements.* Remember, the goal of the session is to help the coachee set clear, concise SMS goals for the next short period of time. Do not allow the session to end without a clear and specifically stated goal.

7) *Asking leading questions.* This is an effective tool for interrogators who want to use a carrot on the end of a stick to get the answers they want to get. It is not effective as a coaching technique. Keep your questions open-ended.

8) *Not remaining objective.* The coachee might feel passionate about a goal that is not really strategic to the team or organizational vision. This especially can be true when organizational change is taking place. It can be difficult to redirect the focus of the goal if you do not maintain your objectivity.

Advice to Meet the Challenge

Don't use the session as an accountability session. The role of a coach is not an accountability partner. Instead, the coach helps the coachee become more accountable to self. Expect a lot from the coachee, keeping in mind that the coaching session is not a performance review or evaluation. Focus on the positive aspects the coachee reveals, identify with the coachee, normalize and personalize without taking over to tell your own story.

Any conversation can become a coaching conversation if you employ these summary three A's:

Active listening

Asking powerful questions

Abstaining from imposing your own plan

Taking a coaching approach to supervision requires that you consider carefully when you should give direction, share an idea, ask a probing question, or remain silent and allow the coachee to come up with their own best course of action. Consider these verses of advice:

- *"Be quick to listen, slow to speak."* (James 1:19)
- *"He who answers before listening—that is his folly and his shame."* (Prov. 18:13)
- *"A fool finds no pleasure in understanding, but delights in airing his own opinions."* (Prov. 18:2)
- "The purposes of a man's heart are deep waters, but a man of understanding draws them out." (Prov. 20:5, NIV)

Putting Together Your Coaching Strategy

Here are two basic models that are easily adaptable to a coaching approach to supervision. The GROW model and the Coaching Conversation both focus on helping the coachee to set a goal and establish a plan for reaching it.

The GROW Model

John Whitmore first introduced the GROW model in leadership coaching in his book *Coaching for Performance*.[26] The four-stage approach includes goal-setting and a thorough evaluation of what it will take to reach the goal. By asking powerful questions, the coach helps to grow the coachee through the four steps of the process:

- **G**oal - What is the goal for the session, for the short and long term? What do you want to work on right now? The goal describes where the coachee wants to be, and so the goal must be stated in very clear terms that will make it obvious to the coachee when the goal has been achieved—specific, measurable and strategic (SMS!)

- **R**eality – What is the current situation? Also, what **R**esources are available to help you reach the goal? Defining the reality leads to a gap analysis to help the coachee determine how far away they are from their goal.

- **O**ptions – "What are all the things you *could* do?" "What alternate strategies or courses of action could be taken?" **O** can also stand for **O**bstacles: "What obstacles do you see that will have to be overcome to reach the goal?" If there were no obstacles, then why would the coachee not already have achieved this? Analysis of different options can include brainstorming to help the coachee start a narrowing process toward choosing the best course of action. Help the coachee to diagnose the need and focus the conversation on moving from the general to a specific action. As you explore options, be sure to identify and align actions with the focus.

- **W**ill – Keep narrowing the focus from *could* do to *want* to and *will* do. "How committed are you to taking action? Do you have the will to do it?" Don't let the coachee get bogged down with "wiggle words." These are words that provide an escape or avoid commitment. ("Maybe I could do this, I might do that, I guess I could...") Help them make a commitment by asking direct questions such as, "So what *WILL* you do and when *WILL* you do it?" or "On a scale of 1 to 10, how committed are you to doing this? What would it take to get your level of commitment to a 10?"

The Coaching Conversation

The coaching conversation model developed by CoachWorks, International, expands the GROW model to a five-step process that also involves goal-setting and analyzing what it will take to reach the goal.[27]

Step 1. Establish the Focus.

This defines the gap between where the coachee is now and where they want to be. Ask the coachee to describe what it will look like when the problem is solved. Help the coachee narrow the problem to focus on goals that are concise, measurable, and attainable (remember, SMS!)

Step 2. Discover Possibilities.

Sometimes we get stuck because we are fixated on one solution. Lead the coachee to brainstorm as many ideas as they can, even if some of these seem far-fetched. Be careful not to shoot down any ideas that the coachee might mention at this time. If they have trouble getting started, ask, "What has worked for you in the past?" or "Tell me about a time when you had success overcoming a similar obstacle." If they are still stuck, ask if it would help if you were to offer a suggestion. Then ask if any other ideas come to mind. If the coachee still cannot produce an option, ask, "Do you know anyone who has faced a similar challenge? Could you ask that person for some advice?"

Step 3. Plan the Action.

Use basic questions to narrow the focus to a specific, *actionable* issue. Start eliminating options that are impractical or unrealistic. Keep personalizing the focus, narrowing down from **possible** options to **real** options, focusing on what the coachee wants to do, can do, and **will** do. Keep asking clarifying questions such as:

"What do you see as most important?"

"Which of these do you want to work on?"

"It sounds like you're saying..."

Step 4. Remove Barriers.

Ask, "What could get in the way of you actually *doing* what you just said you want to do?" Consider what it will take to remove the barriers and then start removing them.

Step 5. Recap.

Ask the coachee to summarize if any new insights have been gained. Questions to ask in the recap might include the following:

- "What was a key insight you got out of this conversation?"
- "What kind of people could best help you meet this goal?"
- "Where can you find them?"
- "Who do you need as an accountability partner?"
- Be sure to ask if they have a clear plan of action: "So what are you going to do and when are you going to do it?"

Wrapping up the Session – Closing Well

The purpose of the coaching session is to help the coachee discover what to do. So the last few minutes should be focused on *action*. Make sure the action is aligned with the focus of the issue the coachee has identified. In the GROW model, these are the WILL questions: "What *will* you do?" In the Coaching Conversation model, this is part of the Recap.

Always pray at the end of the session. Be sure to ask God to keep revealing His plan instead of asking Him to bless *your* plans. Using a coaching approach to supervision is an excellent way to lead the coachee to discover what that plan is and then to follow it.

Coaching Others

While we have focused this chapter on a coaching approach to supervision, the principles we have presented are basic coaching principles that can be applied to any number of relationships or situations. You might find yourself in a peer-to-peer coaching relationship or coaching someone who reports to one of your colleagues. In such cases, it is good to establish an agreement, whether in writing or verbally, that includes the following components:

- *Purpose or objectives of the coaching* – Why coaching? Why now? Is this for a particular project? To become a more effective leader? To address any specific issues or challenges?

- *Expectations* – Clarify what coaching is and how it is different from other relationships. Who will set the focus for each coaching conversation? How will you interact?

- *Confidentiality* – Define the parameters of confidentiality for each of you. How much can each of you share, or not share and with whom?

- *Operating guidelines* – Determine how you are going to work together. How often should you meet and by what means? Face to face, by telephone, video conference or other means? Who will initiate the calls? Any other logistical issues?

- *Commitment* - Set the level of commitment on both sides. How long will you work together? When should you evaluate the coaching relationship to decide on plans for continuing or concluding? Commit to following through with any stated plans or goals.

Assume adult behavior from the coachee. Let the coachee be responsible for taking action. The role of a coach is to be a helper, encouraging the coachee to discover the next steps they need to take to move forward.

Final Challenge

There are many training events and certifications available today for effective coaching. We normally present these principles in a one-day or one and a half-day workshop format to help managers practice and become more comfortable using the basic skills of coaching in their ongoing dialogues with direct reports.

You can coach your people to make good SMS goals that are in tune with the team and organization's goals, objectives, values, and mission without a carrot or a stick. A coaching approach to supervision builds up the coachee and allows them to take responsibility for their own decisions and to carry out their own plan. That is one of the fastest and most reliable ways to get people to buy in, connecting their personal vision, purpose, and goals to those of the team and organization.

At the close of every coaching session we try to wrap up with a series of questions. If I were coaching you right now, I would ask:

So, what are you going to do?
Are you really going to do it?
When are you going to do it?

Coaching Resources and References

(Many of the basic concepts in this chapter were inspired by Jane Creswell's "A Coach Approach to Lead Like Jesus, Workshop" Raleigh, NC, August 2007, based on materials developed by Linda Miller, MCC and Jane Creswell, MCC.)

Collins, Gary, *Christian Coaching: Helping Others Turn Potential into Reality*, 2ND Edition, Navpress Publishing Group, 2009.

Creswell, Jane, *Christ-centered Coaching: 7 Benefits for Ministry Leaders*, Chalice Press, April 2006.

Miller, Linda and Chad Hall, *Coaching for Christian Leaders*, Chalice Press, 2007.

Ogne, Steve and Tim Roehl, *TransforMissional Coaching: Empowering Leaders in a Changing Ministry World*, B&H Books, 2008.

Thomas, Scott and Tom Wood and Steve Brown, *Gospel Coach: Shepherding Leaders to Glorify God*, Zondervan, 2012.

Whitmore, John, *Coaching for Performance: GROWing Human Potential and Purpose - The Principles and Practice of Coaching and Leadership*, 4th Edition, Nicholas Brealey, revised 2009.

Helpful websites:

Center for Creative Leadership, www.ccl.org. (This site has plenty of resources and articles for the development of managers, including many helps on a coaching approach to leadership.)

Coach Approach Ministries, https://coachapproachministries.org/ (CAM posts regular blogs, podcasts and monthly free webinars. Many of these are applicable for supervisors.)

Smith, Lee and Jeannine Sandstrom,
http://www.coachworks.com/ (Coachworks has many
resources for coaching in general.)

Stolfuz, Tony, https://www.coach22.com/ (This site has a
good list of books and other helpful resources.)

Stolfuz, Tony,
http://www.christiancoachingcenter.org/ (We
especially recommend his helps on asking good
questions.)

Webb, Keith, https://keithwebb.com/ (He may show up last
in the alphabetical listing, but Keith provides topnotch
coach training and resources, many of which are free,
including his free guide "Fifty Powerful Coaching
Questions.")

Teaming for Unity
Your Roadmap to More Effective Leadership

"Look for able men from all the people, men who fear God, who are trustworthy and hate a bribe, and place such men over the people as chiefs of thousands, of hundreds, of fifties, and of tens."
Jethro to Moses in Exodus 18:21

"The administrators and the satraps tried to find grounds for charges against Daniel in his conduct of government affairs, but they were unable to do so. They could find no corruption in him, because he was trustworthy and neither corrupt nor negligent."
Daniel 6:4 (NIV)

"Whoever can be trusted with very little can also be trusted with much, and whoever is dishonest with very little will also be dishonest with much. So if you have not been trustworthy in handling worldly wealth, who will trust you with true riches?"
From the Parable of the Shrewd Manager,
Luke 16:10-11 (NIV)

"Do nothing from selfish ambition or conceit, but in humility count others more significant than yourselves. Let each of you look not only to his own interests, but also to the interests of others."
Philippians 2:3-4

> **Servant-stewards build trust by showing their trustworthiness.**
> - Servant-stewards demonstrate their trustworthiness to make good decisions based on knowing right from wrong. (1 Tim. 1:2-4)
> - Servant-stewards do what is right because it is right. (1 Tim. 1:18-20)
> - Servant-stewards stand up for what is right, even when they stand alone. (Titus 2:15)
> - Servant-stewards recognize that they will face opposition/persecution if they are living a godly life. (2 Tim. 3:12-13)
> - Servant-stewards have a clear understanding of their personal core values. (1 Tim. 4:2-3)
> - Servant-stewards inspire confidence in others to do what is right. (2 Tim. 2:3-13)

How to turn a ship around

Often, when leaders want to initiate significant change to increase effectiveness within the organization, they simply say, "We are your leaders. Trust us. This change will be good and will allow us to be much more productive." If you have to tell someone to trust you, it is probably because you sense that they do not trust you and you already see that it will be difficult to get them to follow you where you know the organization needs to go.

Trust does not come automatically with positional leadership. Trust grows out of one's character and is only given to those who have proven themselves to be trustworthy. Trying to initiate massive change without trust will create massive doses of stress at every level of the organization. Eventually, the changes will take place, but at a much higher cost than if trust had been built first. It can be likened to a ship moving forward in one direction at cruising speed when the captain suddenly calls out, "Reverse all engines! Full steam reverse!" Such action might get them going in the opposite direction rapidly, but a lot of people will be picking their teeth out of the bulkhead and the repair bill is going to be astronomical!

On the other hand, if the proper steps are taken in the proper order, the ship can be turned around and headed in the opposite direction with minimal casualties, and the ultimate goal of increased effectiveness and productivity can be reached and sustained for a much longer period. It might take a little more time, but the long-term results will be much more positive. Organizational change and increased organizational effectiveness can only be achieved by following four sequential steps, each of which is dependent on the previous one.[28]

1. Build Character in Yourself (Trustworthiness)

The trustworthiness of individual leaders is the first, essential step toward organizational effectiveness. This is where character is built and core values of the individual are established. Someone has defined character as "who you are when no one else is watching." Leadership is more about character than anything else. The most effective leaders know to "hire character and train for skill."

Our oldest son, Brian, supervised a bi-lingual call center for an insurance company when a corporate head-hunter recommended him to manage a similar center with a fast-growing company based in Atlanta. Brian's department had shown marked improvement by the company's metrics as he experimented with some of the principles he learned from a Lead Like Jesus Encounter.

Although he really wanted to take steps more directly toward a career path in ministry, he agreed to be interviewed by the CEO of the company. Brian knew from the head-hunter that the salary range for this position would be significantly more than he was making at the time.

As the two-hour interview was finally coming to a close, the CEO asked Brian if he had any questions. "Just one," Brian responded. "In all this time you have spent with me you have not asked me one question about my experience. Don't you want to know more about what I have done in my current employment?"

The CEO replied, "Brian, I've spent two hours looking at your character. We can train you to do any job if you have the kind of character we are looking for to build the kind of company we are going to be."

He promised to call on Friday of that same week with his decision. On Thursday, however, Brian called the CEO to withdraw his name from consideration "before you make me an offer that I might not be able to refuse." He explained his desire to continue his studies to prepare for a career in ministry and he did not think this would be the best path to that goal. The CEO tried to convince him that he could still be in bi-vocational part-time ministry. There was even a seminary extension very close to their corporate offices where Brian could work and continue his education. Brian thanked him, but felt he needed to remain true to the commitment he had already made to follow another path.

By the way, just a short time after this, Brian received a call for an initial interview that ultimately led to him being invited to join the First Baptist Church of Montgomery, Alabama, in what he considered to be the dream job he would have hoped to have "someday." He is still there, making a difference twelve years later.

Leadership skills can be learned, but character comes from within. Character traits such as integrity, honesty and trustworthiness are essential to building trust. If there are character flaws in the leader, it will be difficult for the members of the organization to trust and follow that leader to greater levels of effectiveness and productivity in the organization. How many times have you seen someone lose their temper and say something hurtful, and then became apologetic saying, "I'm sorry I acted that way, I'm really not like that." My response to that is, "Oh, yes you are." Your words and behavior are indicators of the character within and when you are under stress, your true character comes to light.

Jesus modeled the importance of establishing his personal leadership, character and trustworthiness before he launched his public ministry. First, he submitted to public baptism by John and then he spent 40 days in the desert where he was tempted by Satan. Both of these actions demonstrated his personal integrity and character that were evidence that he could be trusted as a leader. (Mt. 3:13-4:11) Remember, *being* precedes *doing*. You must first prove yourself to be trustworthy if you want people to trust you.

2. Build Relationships One-on-One and One by One (Trust)

Without the personal integrity of trustworthiness, you cannot be effective at one-on-one leadership where trust is built. After his temptation in the desert, Jesus began to call his disciples, one by one. (Mt. 4:18-22) There is no indication that they joined because they wanted to be part of the band of disciples. Instead, each one of the twelve followed Jesus because *he* invited them to join *him* and they trusted *him* as their leader. Trust and interpersonal relationships are built on the inner core of trustworthiness and personal integrity. If people do not see you consistently demonstrating your trustworthiness, you can forget any hope of being trusted.

Trust in an organization can only be built by trustworthy individuals as they relate to others one-on-one. Obviously, we have to work to build trust, not only in leadership, but also one with another at every level of the organization. Building trust is not easy. It takes time to build trust that can be broken in an instant. Once trust has been broken, it takes even longer to rebuild it, and, in many cases, it can never be fully rebuilt. Keep in mind also that forgiveness is not the same as trust.

The erosion of trust dramatically affects organizational productivity. You can probably imagine people spending time around the "water cooler" complaining and seeking informal counsel about how to deal with a manager or coworker whose trust has been busted. Of course, the modern office "water cooler" might well be text messages, social media, or other electronic means of communication. Demotivated workers will begin spending time and energy looking for "something else." Unwanted attrition will increase and many who stay will be dissatisfied.

Whenever I hear anyone complain about the lack of trust in their organization, I immediately ask, "So what are **you** doing to build trust?" I often get a puzzled look in reaction, especially if the individual is not in top leadership of the organization. Even if you are not in top leadership, you can still play a vital role by proving *you* can be trusted because *you* are trustworthy in *your* interpersonal relations with colleagues, with *your* leaders, and with the people *you* lead. *You* can make a difference!

3. Build Community at the Team Level (Empowerment)

If trust is being built in one-on-one relationships, you can begin building community within the team. Stephen Covey described this as the managerial level where empowerment takes place.[29] Again, if you as the leader have not demonstrated competency at the two previous levels, you cannot effectively empower others and community will not be built. (Refer back to the chapter on "Leading by Serving" for the definition of "empowerment.") Obviously, a leader will not empower someone they do not trust. By like sign, followers will not feel comfortable with their empowered responsibility if they do not feel they can trust their leaders to back them up, support them, and encourage them to succeed. Jesus built community in his disciples as he sent them out two by two to share the good news, heal the sick, raise the dead, cleanse lepers, and cast out demons. (Mt. 10:5-10) By sending them out with such power and authority, he began to build a sense of confidence in them and in each other as they continued to grow as a community of faith.

Even if you do not receive empowerment from your leadership, you can still help the people you lead to feel empowered. For several years our youngest son, Eric, has worked in technical theater and has been a technical director (TD) for two large non-profit theater venues where major Broadway and road show productions took place. As TD, Eric was responsible for communicating with clients of advance shows, ensuring all technical requirements were met, overseeing the work of technical crews, and generally making sure everything went smoothly and safely from load-in to load-out.

In both cases the venue grew in popularity resulting in long seasons when the theater was active seven days a week and for very long days. Eric often worked 16-hour days and went as many as three weeks without a day off. He requested permission to hire an assistant or associate TD to share the responsibility so that a trained person with authority would always be on hand for every production. In both cases the request was flatly denied—multiple times. Unfortunately, in both cases Eric became discouraged after about seven years and eventually had to leave an employment he would have thoroughly enjoyed for several more years if he had felt encouraged and empowered by his employer.

In spite of the fact that Eric did not receive empowerment from his upper management, that did not stop him from empowering the people he supervised. He trained them well and often relied on crew members to do more than their position might ordinarily require. He made sure that they received appropriate time off and defended them to clients and upper management. In some cases, his contract workers might have even made more annual income than he did. We came to know several of his crew members and saw how much they appreciated Eric as their supervisor. They often commented to us how Eric was the best boss they ever had. He understood how to empower people, even when he could not delegate authority to them. And that built strong unity and loyalty in his employees.

4. Build a Culture of Unity (Alignment)

Finally, if the foundation has been laid in steps one, two, and three, you will begin to see the effectiveness of the organization growing through increased alignment. Alignment includes being sure the organization is moving in the right direction to meet its stated purpose and goals as well as the alignment of individual and team goals with the broader goals of the organization. Proper alignment means that the organization, its teams, and its individuals are moving in the same and right direction to meet the stated goals and purpose of the organization. (See the chapter on "Aligning for Advancement.") If there is a general sense in the organization that the entire team has ownership of the goals and cares about accomplishing those goals, there will be a sense of unity that grows out of the community of teams.

After his resurrection, Jesus spent 40 days with his disciples giving them final instructions and reminding them of all he had taught them over the previous three years. As he was about to leave them, he gave them the Great Commission: "*All authority in heaven and on earth has been given to me. Go therefore and make disciples of all nations, baptizing them in the name of the Father and of the Son and of the Holy Spirit, teaching them to observe all that I have commanded you. And behold, I am with you always, to the end of the age.*" (Mt. 28:18-20)

The culture or ethos of an organization is built on the community of teams that grow out of trust relationships that are formed from leaders who are competent, confident, and trustworthy. If leaders have concentrated on steps one, two, and three, then a culture of trust will be built within the organization. That trust will increase as every worker within the organization understands both what they are doing and why. As teams grow to develop their sense of community as part of the larger organization, the trust they feel in their leaders and each other will be transferred to trust in the organization. By the way, when the employees within the organization feel a strong sense of trust in their leaders and community within their teams, it will also affect the relationships with customers, clients, or end-users who will see the company as reliable and trustworthy. And that will lead to greater effectiveness and productivity for the organization as a whole.

Our second son, Robert, has worked with office furniture installation companies for several years. Robert is a hands-on man with managerial strengths that show up clearly in his personality profile. He was doing a very good job as lead installer but was not feeling valued by the company. Whenever there was an opening for a promotion, Robert was passed over, even though he was probably the best qualified applicant for a project manager position because they felt they could not afford to lose his skills as an installer. Although he received some increase in salary, he felt under-valued and over-used by the company that was impeding his personal and occupational growth.

The company management's failure to build an ethos of investing in the growth of its employees ultimately led Robert to feel distrust and dissatisfaction with his employment. In the end, however, that might have been a good thing for Robert. He left that company to become a partner in a new startup business.

As a leader in the new company, Robert sees the value of succession planning and encouraging his employees to grow in their aspirations. He had to start out as lead installer for his own company, but quickly began to identify who could fill that role to allow him to fill other essential needs for the growing business.

No Shortcuts

Leaders often want to take a shortcut to try and increase organizational effectiveness, but the leadership road is one-way only and to get to this level, you must build on the previous three levels. You cannot achieve organizational alignment and maximum effectiveness if you have not built the organization on the DNA of trust that grows out of an intrinsic trustworthiness that demonstrates a willingness to empower individuals throughout the organization. Each level must build on the previous one. Increased effectiveness in the organization will also foster the growth of personal leadership and character development in the people who make up the organization—which takes us right back to step one!

One-Way Communication is Not Enough.

Systemic problems in every organization seem to always include communication problems within the organization. One of the main reasons communication breaks down is lack of trust. And lack of communication further breaks down trust. This is true both in interpersonal relations and in organizational structure. The vicious cycle is hard to break.

Even if communication is flowing freely within the organization, if it is not also accompanied by a large dose of empowerment and community building at every level, the workers will develop a sense of frustration to the point that they will conclude that it might be better to not communicate. Empowerment and community are developed at the team level and, again, the heart of the solution is in the issue of trust.

If people feel they can communicate in an environment of mutual trust, there will be three long-term results: 1) improvement in job satisfaction; 2) greater alignment between individual and organizational goals; and 3) increased productivity and organizational effectiveness.

You need to TRI harder

What makes you feel valued in your workplace? We have asked a number of people that question, and it seems to come down to three things:

    Trust
    Respect and
    Input

Trust: "assured reliance on the character, ability, strength, or truth of someone or something." (Merriam-Webster)

As a leader, you want your followers to trust you, but to gain their trust, you must first prove yourself to be trustworthy. One way to build trustworthiness is to place trust in the other person. The more trust I show you, the more I increase the likelihood that you will trust me. Delegation of responsibility is a huge way to build trust. Sharing of information, vulnerability, openness, and sharing personal prayer requests are also trust builders.

Respect: "a feeling of deep admiration for someone or something elicited by their abilities, qualities, or achievements." (Oxford Dictionary)

Recognition of the other person's experience, contributions, or individual accomplishments can go a very long way toward making the person feel respected. Providing your undivided attention to the other person also displays respect for their time and thoughts. A simple way to do that is don't allow yourself to be distracted by text messages, emails, or other calls when speaking with them.

Input: "advice or opinions that help someone make a decision." (Merriam-Webster)

This is about feeling you have the opportunity to share **Information** and **Insights**. Being given the opportunity to share these three I's creates a feeling of **empowerment.**

$$\text{Information} \times \text{Input} \times \text{Insight} = \text{Empowerment}$$
$$(I^3 = E)$$

The opportunity to give **input** up line with absolute confidence that they will be heard makes people feel they actually make a difference. This is more than just having the opportunity to influence decisions. It has to do with simply being heard, knowing that your manager has an open ear and will give attention to what you have to share—even if your idea is not implemented.

The ability to give input also helps to build trust that leads to respect. Of course, if a person's input is repeatedly rejected outright, then that becomes a trust-buster, making the person feel disrespected and devalued. You can always acknowledge the person's input with thanks, and if appropriate, offer a brief explanation of why you did not follow the suggestion.

All of this boils down to helping people feel that they are persons of worth, that they are known and valued for who they are and not just for what they do. Who you are amounts to much more than just what you do in your job at work.

Don't Pull the Decision Trigger Too Soon

All too often leaders pull the trigger on the decision gun too quickly. The decision has been made, money spent, changes initiated, and emotional capital expended within the work force only to discover that the price of this decision was much too high and the desired results did not materialize. Why? What could have been done to avoid this disaster?

Several years ago, someone gave me a button that says, "Don't Confuse Me with the Facts." For years I have kept that button hanging around the neck of a Tweety Bird pen holder in a prominent place on my desk. It serves to remind me how important it is to listen to the people I lead and not assume that I already know what is best for the organization in all cases. Sometimes my intuition and my forward thinking can get us all into trouble if I ignore the facts that others can see clearly from their perspective.

When the I's Don't Carry the Vote

Have you ever been in a situation where you knew your boss was about to make a huge mistake? The decision had already been made, but you knew it would not succeed. This was not just a hunch or intuition. You had specific information that, if it were seriously considered, could alter the decision and the results. Perhaps you were reluctant to offer your suggestion for fear of being rejected. You did not want to appear to be promoting yourself or you did not want to be accused of insubordination or not being a team player by speaking up against what the boss wanted. So, you remained silent. You might have ventured to mention your thoughts to one or two close associates, or your spouse. Then, when the decision had been finalized, action taken, policies put in place, and the results were less than successful, you said to yourself (or to the trusted few with whom you had shared your insights), "I knew this would happen."

There are times when leaders must make unpopular decisions for the greater good of the larger organization. After I have given my input and shared my information and insight, the leader might decide to go ahead with the decision as he has planned, choosing not to act on my suggestions. In such cases, I can assume that the leader has received information from other sources and is giving more weight to their input than he gives to mine or that the leader has considered my input, but he has other reasons for setting my information aside. Although I may not agree with the final decision, I will submit to his authority and do my best to make it succeed because I know that I have done my part by not withholding information that could have helped make a better decision

Leadership Hints

Imagine what your organization would look like if leaders would go out of their way to demonstrate a genuine value for every worker at every level throughout the organization. What could you do to start building such an organization right now? What could you do to show that you are genuinely **TRI**-ing? (Remember, **T**rust, **R**espect, **I**nput.)

Since the essence of leadership is influencing others, the best leaders become experts at developing and maintaining good interpersonal skills. While you need the people you lead to help you reach your own goals and the objectives of your organization, remember they are not just objects or resources to be used. They are people who need to feel valued and respected. They will follow your leadership if they trust you to lead them to fulfill their personal visions and goals as they contribute to the goals and objectives of the organization. (More about that later in the chapter on "Aligning for Advancement.")

Take a risk and invite input from the people you lead. Try not to become defensive or overly sensitive when the suggestions seem contrary to the action you had planned. Thank them for their input, even if you are not able to implement every suggestion. Give genuine praise for suggestions that make a positive difference, but don't place blame if the final decision does not produce the desired effect. Let them know you want to make the best decisions for the good of the organization and that you truly value their input, even if you cannot always act on every suggestion. If followers feel their input has been heard and considered, they are much more likely to support the decision, even if their suggestions are not incorporated into the final decision. Keep the door open for more input, information, and insights. Let their "I's" be your eyes to help you see how to make better decisions.

Followership Hints

Every leader is also a follower. Even if you are not feeling valued at work, you can make others feel valued. Consider starting your own campaign by showing respect for your manager or supervisor. Offer your input with an attitude of helping. Remember also that your attitude extends beyond the workplace. Would your family members say they feel valued by you? Would they say you are **TRI**-ing at home?

Take a risk and ask if you can provide input with information that might help your leader make the best decision. Let your leader know you want them to succeed. If you do not receive credit for the idea, remember that someone else could be giving similar information and insight from another perspective that coincides with yours. If the leader chooses not to follow your suggestions, remember that they also receive input, information, and insight from other sources. Give the benefit of the doubt and assume that your leader wants to make the best decisions for the good of the organization. Once the decision is made, do everything you can to make it succeed. Remember, the best leaders are also good followers, so be a good follower!

Trust and communication are two-way streets. As a follower, you might not feel comfortable addressing your leader with issues and problems. You might even assume that the leader does not want to hear your input. The follower's input is essential to help leaders make better decisions. If the leader has a blind side and you are not willing to address that issue with your leader, then trust in the leader will erode and both you and others in the organization will suffer. Take a risk to talk to your leader about issues that affect trust.

> **Servant-stewards have an observably close walk with the Lord.**
> - Servant-stewards act with appropriate confidence giving evidence of the fruit of the Spirit in every aspect of their daily lives. (2 Tim. 1:7; 1 Tim. 1:2-4)
> - Servant-stewards demonstrate a biblical understanding of Christ as the center. Their focus is on Christ and not on self. (1 Tim. 1:16-17)
> - Servant-stewards continually seek to grow in their own faith and self-awareness of their strengths and liabilities. (2 Tim. 2:20-21)

Practical Assignment

Take a personal retreat and reflect on who you are, whose you are, and what you need to do to develop your character and build trust. How trustworthy do you think people consider you to be? What can you do to prove your trustworthiness, grow trust in the organization, build community in your team, and contribute to the general effectiveness of your organization?

Use Assessments to Help Build Unity

Regardless of their level of development, everyone needs to receive some form of affirmation from their supervisor. One reason supervisors fail to give affirmations is because they really don't know the people they are supervising. Assessments can help, but simply administering assessments will not increase the productivity of an individual or team. Unless the assessment leads to some lasting action that brings significant positive change to benefit the individual, the team, and the organization, then you really are not getting the full value of the time and money being spent on it. When we suggest the use of assessments for teambuilding, some leaders will balk at the idea because they have seen little or no lasting value from the insights provided by previous assessments they have used. Even when a workshop has been fun and the team members have gotten new insights to their behaviors, all too often the reports go on a shelf with little to no lasting change taking place.

As mentioned previously, assessments are only tools. If you know how to use the results of the assessment over a period of time, the assessment can help to give valuable insights that can lead to significant change for healthier, more productive individuals and teams.

We have found the following assessments to be the most effective for building unity in teams. Each of these requires a team coach to get the most benefit from them.

The Birkman Method. As we mentioned in the chapter on "Supervising for Success," the Birkman is a premier assessment for building both self-awareness and social awareness, providing an in-depth understanding of who we are naturally and highlighting how we effectively engage with those around us. Team building workshops using The Birkman provide a common language to begin a healthy dialogue to discuss personality in the workplace through the use of Birkman symbols, colors, and component names. This common language can easily become a part of an organizational culture so that you have a non-judgmental way to discuss stylistic differences that can be assets or challenges for the team. Productivity of the team increases as leaders learn to celebrate each team member's strengths and make work assignments that more closely match individuals' interests. [30]

Grip-Birkman for faith-based groups. Adding *Your Leadership Grip* to The Birkman Method gives insight to your supernatural design through three lenses: your spiritual gift combination, your preferred style of working in a team setting, and the roles you play to help build the Body of Christ. We have also used Your Leadership Grip or Grip-Birkman (the powerful combination of Your Leadership Grip and The Birkman Method) with Christian business leaders to help them see how their Spiritual Gifts, preferred Team Styles, and Body-Building Roles affect the way they interact with others in their work environment that cannot fully be explained by their natural personality alone. [31]

Style Matters (the Kraybill Conflict Style Inventory). Like most conflict mode assessments, Kraybill's version is built on the Managerial Style Grid (Mouton-Blake Grid) developed by Jane Mouton and Robert Blake in the 1960's. The simple questionnaire takes about 15 minutes to complete. It provides answers for what Kraybill calls "calm" and "storm" conditions, noting that our styles may change under stress. *Style Matters* works very well in combination with The Birkman Method or Grip-Birkman to help team members see how their personality and spiritual gifts can affect the way they deal with conflict. Kraybill has also developed helps that distinguish between low context (individualist) and high context (collectivist) cultures and how people deal differently with conflict based on their culture.[32]

Our purpose here is not to sell you on using these assessments. If something else works for you, by all means use it. Since, however, these are the three assessments we have found to be the most effective in our team-building and coaching practice, our illustrations will refer to these.

Personalize Incentives

You need to discover what will motivate your people to feel valued by the organization. Birkman calls this the Incentives Component of behavior. Most people are basically team-oriented and can focus on long-term rewards as motivation. Our society has drilled into us that we ought to be team-minded, and most people would say they usually are okay with team rewards. (Giant stadiums full of sports fans wearing their team colors bear that out!) At the same time, they have a strong hidden need for an environment which rewards individual achievement. Under stress, these people may become self-promotional and overly competitive if this need is not met.

Other people are more competitive as they look for opportunities to get ahead and need an environment that supports and rewards their individual effort. Under stress these people may lose trust in others and take self-protective actions if they don't get the personal recognition and rewards for their accomplishments.

A final group will appear trustful and focused on fairness in dealing with others. People in this last group need to work in an area that is focused on team achievement as a reward system. They honestly do not want the individual attention as they have a stronger need for everyone on the team to win together. These people are likely to feel stressed if they are singled out for what they think is unnecessary personal recognition or when they are forced to negotiate individual rewards (such as salary raises). When that happens, they might become idealistic and give in to those who are trying to take advantage of the system.

Keep in mind that it is not about the money. Even for highly motivated salespeople with a high "Incentives" need, money is just one way of "keeping score." There are other ways to help fuel their healthy competitiveness.

Unfortunately, non-profit organizations don't tend to do well at rewarding individuals for a job well-done. They usually can't provide incentive raises or bonuses. Many attempts to give personal recognition fall flat, either because the individual knows everyone gets the same thing (such as automatic longevity increases in salary) or one person gets called up to the stage to be verbally honored for something they did not accomplish alone or that was not unique to them.

Be creative as you try to find other ways to give appropriate tangible rewards to help keep people motivated. Here are a few ideas of incentives that do not have to be very costly.

1. Say "thank you" when they do great work.
2. Make sure they're using the best equipment.
3. Honor your best personnel publicly. (Be specific about *why* they are being honored.)
5. Give them an extra vacation day that doesn't count against any policy limits.
6. Take them out for a long lunch.
7. Give them the option of a flexible work schedule.
8. Give away outside services, coupons or gift cards.
9. Let them discard a project that's weighing them down.
10. Make a fun game out of the gifts. Place the rewards in a box and let them draw out their reward.[33]

Keep them "Interested" in their Job

Most new jobs are assigned based on skill. We tend to look at past performance, in search of someone who has already shown that they can do this job. However, someone can be very good at something they are not really interested in. Over time, this can erode the overall motivation for the job because the worker is executing an assignment they merely *can* do, not one they *want* to do or *like* to do.

Imagine how productive a team member might be if, when making your assignments, you could balance the skill needed for the task with the motivational needs of the worker. Skills can be learned. Motivation, however, comes from within the individual. There will be times when the urgency of the task requires an experienced person to get the job done. Looking to a long-term solution, however, you will be better served if you know the person's interests. Someone may volunteer for an assignment you don't think they are qualified for. Consider if they might be volunteering because this is something they really want to do—something that will not drain them but will actually energize them as they do the task. They will be more likely to invest the time and energy in building the skills needed to do the job well when the task is something that motivates them. It is easier to train them to do the task than to motivate someone else to keep doing it when they aren't already motivated by their interest in it. The self-motivated person is more likely to stay committed to the assignment longer, with more enthusiasm and higher productivity than the person who has the skill without the motivational need.

The Birkman Method measures ten general categories of Interests and shows a percentile rating for the individual's relative interest in each category. This becomes a measure of one's motivation that can affect their attitude.

For example, a team member who has a high "Outdoor" score will be drained of energy fairly quickly if you give them an assignment as a customer service rep who spends all day on the phone, looking at a computer screen in a cubicle with no outside windows. They might have demonstrated all the characteristics you want in that position such as friendliness, lots of patience, and familiarity with the company's products, policies and procedures. But they will be drained of energy at the end of the day and will soon be demotivated to do the job well for very long.

Another team member might have a high "Numbers" score. While other team members groan at the prospect of completing financial reports and budgets, this person might be whistling as they happily work with spreadsheets tucked away in their own little corner office. You get the idea.

On the other hand, very low Birkman Interest scores will indicate aversions—things that will quickly demotivate the person. You can't make every task assignment based on interests alone. We all have some tasks associated with our work that fall outside our natural interests. You can't allow a person to use their Birkman Interests as a "Get out of Jail Free" card just because of a low Interest score. A person can, however, use the Birkman to build balance in their life. If a significant majority of your time is spent involved in activities that match your interests and motivate you, then you can use the energy gained from these to do the uninteresting other stuff that has to be done. We have known many people who found that balance through hobbies or other activities outside their work environment. People we have coached report a huge difference in energy and motivation when they find ways to incorporate their highest Interests into their lives on a regular basis.

Spiritual Gifts at Work

We tend to think of spiritual gifts as only having a place in church ministry—"Should I teach a children's class or serve on the Benevolence Committee?" But you don't check your gifts at the door as you leave Sunday worship. Sometimes you might find that someone you supervise has an unusually effective way of getting the job done that is outside their natural personality or strength (Usual Style as described by their Birkman report). You can't fully understand their behavior without considering their giftedness. In making job and task assignments, what if we added spiritual gifts to the mix?

Often in team-building workshops, we see individuals who clearly have hidden or undeveloped gifts that the team needs, but their current assignment has not taken their gifts into consideration. If you want a truly energized worker, try helping them find a way to apply both their interests and their gifts to their job. That's when you are likely to hear, "I can't believe they actually pay me to do this!" (By the way, don't stop paying them!)

We also tend to think of gifts as being given to specific individuals. That is only partially true. The gifts are given to the individuals in the Body of Christ for the building up of the Body as a whole so that together we can glorify God. (Rom. 12:4-5; 1 Cor. 12:12-27; Eph. 4:1-16; 1 Pet. 4:10-11) As one workshop participant put it, "We have a pronoun problem!" Paul Ford describes it as a need to move our thinking from "I" to "We." He developed the spiritual gifts inventory, *Your Leadership Grip,* with the concept that the only way to fully understand your gifts is in the context of body life. He expanded the concept in his later work, *Moving from I to We:*

> As people discern, exercise, and grow in their spiritual gifts, they begin to minister through the power of the Holy Spirit. That is, after all, what using your spiritual gifts means — allowing the power of the Holy Spirit to work through you for the common good. This is not really about leadership training, but rather about stewarding various gifts and roles... As the Spirit of God is manifested in the gathering of believers and speaks through some to encourage others, a dynamic dimension is added. The body truly grows and builds itself up in love.[34]

The Importance of Affirmations

A major task as a supervisor is to create a support system for personnel which provides the necessary physical, intellectual, spiritual, financial, emotional, and personal support they need. Providing a way of affirming those being supervised can be one of the most important parts of such a support system.

In our team-building workshops, we have learned the immeasurable value of affirmations to help build team unity. Throughout the workshop, the coach leads team members to be vulnerable as they share insights from their personal profiles and experiences and invites the group to affirm each person after they have shared. At the close of each workshop, after team members have begun to become comfortable with the language and feel a certain degree of trust in their teammates, we gather the group in a circle and spend time allowing the people in the group to affirm each participant.

A trained coach guides the group through the process, instructing them to use only positive words to express genuine affirmation or appreciation for something about the individual who is the current focus of affirmation. No sarcasm and no "backhanded" complements are allowed (such as "I used to think you were a real jerk, but now I see you might actually have some redeeming qualities.") The individual receiving the affirmation must remain silent (except to possibly say "Thank you") and receive each affirmation graciously. Disagreeing or rejecting the affirmation is not allowed. The expression of affirmations is voluntary and random and range from one word descriptors (e.g. "Encourager") to several phrases with examples. For some people, this has been the first time they have ever experienced anything like this, so we always try to have a box of tissues handy. This is a time to express genuine appreciation for the gifts and strengths of each team member and can be a powerful tool for building unity in the group.

We encourage supervisors and team leaders to continue the practice of expressing affirmations regularly in team meetings. Teams that meet more frequently might select one or two individuals to affirm each time to avoid allowing it to become a routine practice. The point is to provide a genuine celebration of each team member's contribution to make this team better at their assignment as part of the entire organization fulfilling its mission.

How to Lead Great Team Meetings

The way you lead team meetings can make or break your team's morale. Many team leaders don't even realize how they are demoralizing their team members by the decision-making process in team meetings. Team meetings become morale busters when team members feel:

- Powerless to make any decisions as individuals or as a group.
- Encouraged to contribute to the discussion only to have their input ignored and the decision to be made autocratically by the leader.
- Frustrated when decisions that appeared to have been made by the group are changed or replaced by the leader after the meeting.

We had a leader once who decided staff meetings were a waste of time. Every week, the main focus of the meeting was on who had not done what he had assigned in the last meeting. He finally became as frustrated as the rest of us already were and put an end to the meetings. That was a shame because we had some very talented people who could have contributed to make some great decisions.

So how can you make team meetings great and not a chore that everyone dreads? Start by making sure the agenda is agile and focused on what everyone considers important. Some team leaders prefer to have everything on the agenda ahead of time so they can print it out and follow it strictly. The problem is that something always comes up unexpectedly or grows out of the discussion in the meeting.

Share ownership of the agenda

Before the meeting starts, be sure someone is assigned to keep a task list. Don't try to keep detailed minutes of the meeting. Just keep a running list of the decisions made and who is the responsible actor for each decision.

We like to follow a two-step process to set the agenda:

Step 1. List and Prioritize. First, list all the agenda items that everyone wants to add and write these on a white board (or shared screen for remote teams). Going around the room each team member shares any items to add to the list and assigns a priority level to each item as they share it:

> *Priority 1* items are urgent and require a decision before the meeting is over.

> *Priority 2* items are important and need input from the group before a final decision can be made.

> *Priority 3* items are not urgent but would be nice to discuss and brainstorm if there is time after dealing with the higher priority issues. Some priority 3 items might be looking to the future and some of these might become priority 1 or 2 later.

Step 2. Categorize. As each item comes up for discussion, ask the person who mentioned this agenda item to categorize the type of decision that will be required.

1. *Collaborative.* Is this a decision that the group should make by consensus?
2. *Consultative.* Is this a decision you can and will make after receiving input from the group?
3. *Informative.* Is this a decision that you are making and you are simply informing the

group of your decision and reasons for making it?

4. *Delegative.* Is this a decision that touches someone else's area of responsibility such that the decision should be delegated to them?
5. *Directive.* Is this a decision the team leader needs to make?

When a team first begins using this process, they might have trouble deciding what type of decision is needed for some agenda items. Asking the above questions usually is enough for most people to decide what category of decision an item will require. Occasionally, you as the leader might need to declare the category for an item. Try to share the decision process as much as you possibly can.

Start with the most important items first

Group items that seem to be connected, and then start with the most important tasks first. As you discuss each item, you might well discover that other agenda items are connected. Don't feel bound to put these off until you get to them. Problem solving is rarely a linear process. Often the solution to one problem can be a linchpin to solving several issues. Allow the discussion to flow naturally. Check off items as they are covered. We have often been in meetings where the last items on the list were wiped off the board because they were solved within the discussion of bigger issues.

Recap the decisions that are made

At the close of the meeting, ask the recorder to read the decision list and responsible parties for each decision. Clarify or make any adjustments to assignments as needed. Send the entire list to everyone, including any team members who were not present.

Reduced Workforce Issues

Most organizations are much better at adding new innovations than they are at eliminating old structures. When management decides it needs to downsize and reduce the number of employees to save money, it is unreasonable to expect the remaining personnel to "take up the slack," although that is the continuing trend. People might be willing to do that for an interim period until the replacement is found, but the leak in the barrel will soon widen as more people feel under-appreciated and decide the only way to get relief is to leave. Overloading people with unrealistic expectations to keep producing at the same level without the same number of personnel is like Pharaoh demanding that the Hebrews keep making the same number and quality of bricks but adding the work of gathering their own straw.[35] You just can't do that for very long before people start burning out and leaving.

<u>Leadership Hints</u>

So, what's the solution when upper management has dictated a reduction in personnel or put a freeze on hiring? Look for things *not* to do. Ask the team for input: "Are there things that we have been doing that might have served a very good purpose in the past, but really are not that necessary right now? Are there any tasks or projects that need to be put on hold for now?" Don't make the decision arbitrarily. The perspective of those who are actually doing the tasks is essential. You might think something is not so important while they might see very valid reasons to keep doing it to avoid problems farther down the road. On the other hand, they might have a list of tasks that are in the 80% category of energy expended for the 20% return (or even less!)

Find ways to acknowledge and reward a good job for everyone who is feeling the pressure. Instead of working longer hours every day, make sure everyone is getting time off for rest and recreation. You really ought to do all this even when there is no reduction in the workforce. Refer to the section on margin and overload in the chapter on "Leading by Serving."

Do everything you can to make sure they feel they are appreciated as the most important resource your company has—because they are! Remember your stewardship responsibility for the people you have been given to lead.

Building Cohesive Virtual Teams

Let's face it. Virtual teams are going to be the norm in many places for the foreseeable future. The concept of a cohesive virtual team, however, might seem to be a contradiction of terms. Is it even accurate to call people who are scattered across multiple countries and time zones a "team"? The term "virtual" has come to be equated with anything that is communicated by electronic means. The original meaning of the word, however, is "being such in power, force, or effect, though not actually or expressly such."[36] In other words, it may look like it, but *it is not really real*. As some old-timers from my youth used to say, "Almost nearly, but not quite hardly." In reality, most "virtual" teams are not really teams at all. In many cases, they might be at best a workgroup, but often the reality will be that the individuals are really independent operators who happen to have the same supervisor.

So perhaps the real challenge is not so much in building a cohesive team as it is about helping you as a manager to build trust, improve morale, and motivate your people through every available communication medium. Most of the time, your communication will necessarily be by electronic media for your people living and working in distant, remote, or isolated locations. When working with remote teams, the most important task for a supervisor is to manage the individuals in such a way that they feel valued and supported in their efforts to contribute to the organization's goals, vision, and mission. Here are some tips about how to effectively supervise people from a distance.

Tips for Supervising from a Distance

Not everyone is suited for isolation.

This is probably the most important tip of all. Newly recruited personnel might think they have what it takes to live and work independently apart from other team members, but many times the reality of isolation and the lack of frequent direct contact with a supervisor leads to floundering and failure. People in isolated assignments should already have demonstrated the following traits:

- Self-motivated: possesses a strong sense of drive and the ability to work independently
- Socially Confident: able to get out, initiate contacts with other people and make new friends easily
- Organized: plan-oriented and organizes work in an efficient and easily accessible way
- Disciplined: manages time wisely and avoids distractions to ensure work is completed on time
- Focused: not easily distracted
- Assertive: knows when and how to speak up with concerns and suggestions
- Tech-savvy: comfortable using different platforms for communication
- Confident: does not require close oversight or constant approval to continue doing well [37]

The people best suited for remote assignments are those who can be comfortable relating to people one-on-one. Remote workers who need a group environment to "recharge" will have to find or build their own groups within the community where they live and work. If they need a great deal of social interaction or oversight, they should not work remotely and they will be dissatisfied and less effective if forced into isolated remote work

Face-to-face meetings are still necessary.

Everyone who has written anything about virtual teams seems to agree on this point: face-to-face, real-live meetings are vitally necessary for virtual teams to succeed. In their research on the subject, Rick Lepsinger and Darleen DeRosa found that "Poor communication, lack of engagement, and lack of attention during virtual meetings are a few of the warning signs that a high-touch environment has not been achieved. While meeting face-to-face requires time and expense, virtual teams who invest in one or two such meetings per year perform better overall than those who do not."[38] In addition to regular group meetings, site visits by the supervisor can be a powerful boost to morale. Also encourage team members to visit each other on site and share in-person collaboration on some projects. This provides an "iron sharpening iron" or cross-pollination environment that may be missing in the team members' development (and does not require the supervisor's presence)!

Adjust your leadership style to recognize the different challenges.

Good leadership is good leadership, regardless of whether you are in the same office every day or separated by thousands of miles. The difference distance makes is the need to do more of the same good things. Be more deliberate and intentional about scheduling regular meetings. Focus even more on being authentic, building relationships and trust, connecting with team members, and connecting them with each other.

Over-communicate.

Often virtual team members will feel they are "out of sight, out of mind." Electronic communication is, by nature, less personal than face-to-face and often masks the non-verbal communication. To compensate for this, you need to make an effort to communicate more—both more frequently and with more information using a variety of media (phone, email, instant messaging, texting, virtual media, web conferences, video conferencing, others). This can be tricky, given the fact that we are in the age of information overload. More frequent shorter messages are more effective than long messages with multiple sub-points.

At the same time, information gets scattered through multiple media and people can have trouble locating information again. Establish and maintain an "official" communication channel, such as a company email domain. Following up a web meeting with a personal email outlining the pertinent points from the meeting and a personal message to each participant can be a powerful way to reinforce what was decided and also to encourage each person in their assignment.

Practice active listening and listen more intently, since the non-verbal communication is more limited. Ask more questions, using a coaching approach as much as possible. If you think you are already over-communicating, you are probably just beginning to communicate well.[39]

Keep it as personal as possible.

Make regular one-on-one contact to talk about more than their work responsibilities. Ask about their day, how they are feeling, and how other family members are. Remember that everyone has a life outside of work. Family issues and life stresses affect every aspect of our lives. Schedule one-on-one time with each individual whenever the team is together. Take time at the beginning of every meeting (virtual or in person) to connect on a personal basis. Encourage early arrivers for web meetings to chat informally with each other. Don't be concerned if they are talking about the weekend football games, hobbies, or achievements of their children or grandchildren. Do be concerned, however, if all they ever talk about is work. As team members get to know each other, trust is built and strong bonds will grow between members, increasing morale and effectiveness.

Encourage members to communicate with each other on their own.

Set up "virtual water coolers."

One thing that virtual teams miss is the opportunity for spontaneity that often occurs with co-located teams. Consider how you might create "virtual water coolers" to encourage more informal communication. Encourage all team members, remote and onsite, to participate in closed social media chats by setting up private groups. Encourage team members to informally share with one another. Occasionally check in as a participant. This is not the place to issue directives, but for informal conversation. Be careful not to use this as a means of monitoring, snooping, or trying to catch people bad-mouthing you or the organization. Be careful also not to allow yourself to be dragged into a gripe session. Don't get defensive or up on a soapbox if any conversations turn to any of your potential hot buttons.

Maintain a high standard of behavior during virtual meetings.

Because distractions and interruptions are so frequent during conference calls (and so annoying to the other participants), each member needs to make a commitment to the other participants to stay even more focused on the conversation than they might during a live in-person meeting. Strongly encourage (or gently insist) that everyone use headsets and microphones to minimize feedback loops. This will also eliminate the need to use the mute button which will allow more spontaneous conversation. Leaving the mics open and live can help the flow of the conversation to be more natural, instead of having to wait for the "Oops. I'm sorry, my mic was muted." It will also cut back on those embarrassing accidental slips when someone might have thought the mic was muted, but it wasn't. Participants can express verbal approvals (or disapprovals) when someone makes a point instead of passively remaining silent which can be misinterpreted either way. There will still be the need to speak one at a time and to not interrupt each other. Establish a set of meeting rules and share these with all the participants.

Build relationships by building trust.

Strong relationships are critical for any team, and especially for virtual team members, to get everyone on the same page and rowing in the same direction. Strong relationships are built on trust. Most researchers agree that trust among geographically distributed team members is measured almost exclusively by reliability. On the one hand, the remote worker builds trust from you when you as the supervisor see them as a reliable worker who is focusing on the right things to be effective in the work assignment. On the other hand, you build trust from them as you demonstrate your reliability. Be available and accessible to your supervisees. Let them know that they can count on you to get them the help they need to do the job they have been assigned. Keeping appointments and calling on time shows you to be reliable. Answering email promptly can be a reliability/trust builder. Failure to answer can equally be a reliability/trust-eroder. Keep in mind that the email you are reading is the personal representative of a real live person who generated it.

Trust is also increased by being transparent. Share the rationale behind your decisions and actions. Let remote team members in on your thought process, even before a decision is final. (Be sure to make it clear when this is something you are thinking about and have not yet decided. Some people will mistake a statement such as, "I'm thinking about..." to mean "This is what we are going to do.") Give frequent updates to let people know how and why the thought is progressing or if it has been set aside. Share personal information to build the relationship. Include some of your own personal challenges, but be careful not to "gripe down."[40]

Work to increase your emotional intelligence.

Some people have a naturally high emotional intelligence quotient (EI or EQ). These people are naturally gifted with self-awareness and other-awareness. They can easily read other people's emotions and can connect with them on a deeper level than just using words to communicate. Emotional intelligence involves five essential elements:

- **Self-awareness** – knowing how you feel and how your emotions and your actions can affect the people around you, knowing your personal strengths and weaknesses.
- **Self-regulation** – being able to stay calm without verbally attacking others, stereotyping people, making emotional decisions or compromising your values. Accepting responsibility for mistakes or when something goes wrong.
- **Internal Motivation** – enjoying what you do and actively pursuing goals with optimism.
- **Empathy** – having the ability to put yourself in someone else's situation, challenge others who are acting unfairly, give constructive feedback, and practice active listening.
- **Social skills** – being a good communicator, able to work with a wide variety of personalities, diplomatic in dealing with conflict. [41]

The more adept one is at managing each of these areas, the higher one's emotional intelligence. Supervisors with lower emotional intelligence will have more challenges dealing with people through indirect means of communication. Your emotional intelligence can, however, be increased if you are willing to work on it.

Aligning for Advancement
Connecting Organizational Vision
to Personal Vision

"When we are no longer able to change a situation,
we are challenged to change ourselves."
(Victor Frankl)

"The only human institution
which rejects progress is the cemetery."
(Harold Wilson)

"So we rebuilt the wall...
for the people worked with all their heart."
(Nehemiah 4:6)

Organizational Change Stress Syndrome

Whenever any organization makes a major change, many of its workers will experience symptoms of what we call "Organizational Change Stress Syndrome" (OCSS). Don't bother looking it up in the *Diagnostic and Statistical Manual of Mental Disorders.*[42] The certainty of its existence, nonetheless, is supported by the evidence of increased stress in the lives of people within the organization, from top level management to part-time volunteers and everyone in between.

Too much change in too short a time produces a shock to the individual's ability to absorb, assimilate, and adapt. As the speed of change increases, individuals experience high levels of stress and the inability to adapt quickly enough. This results in reduced productivity and quality of work. In the late 1960s and early 1970s Alvin Toffler first described this phenomenon as what he called "future shock." Toffler observed that an extremely high degree of future shock can eventually lead to such symptoms as malicious compliance, overt blocking of the organization's tasks, covert undermining of organizational leadership, or promotion of negativity among other workers.[43]

Toffler also coined the term "information overload." Information overload can compound OCSS. People want concrete information from their leaders, and the message from leadership needs to be stated clearly and repeatedly for it to be effectively absorbed and integrated into the organization's ethos. At the same time, information overload will compound the effects of OCSS when the communications about changes are coming at a faster pace than the organization's health and resilience can handle.

Long after the changes are instituted, a number of people within the organization will still seem to be struggling with prevailing questions that are asked in a number of different ways.

- How do we get more people on board with the needed changes?
- If this change was so great, then why are we still floundering in many areas?
- If we all really believe in the vision, why don't we see significant increases in our effectiveness and productivity?
- Why does it take so long to complete the change?
- Why can't we go back to the way things were?
- Why do some people have to leave the organization to follow their dreams or calling?
- What are we really here for anyway?
- What will it take to make the vision reality?

OCSS affects people at every level in the organization—even those who initiate the changes. Once the changes begin, there are always unforeseen adjustments that must be made. It can be like remodeling a house: once you start ripping out drywall, floors, and ceilings you never know what you may find underneath. And the cost is always more than you anticipated!

I started tracking the number of changes in personnel that were set in motion when a mid-level manager was asked to fill a new position in the organization we were serving at the time. That simple change in structure resulted in a total of at least fourteen individuals changing job assignments or having to move over the course of the next two years before the ripple effect finally subsided. And that's not counting the number of people the manager moved or reassigned once he started his new position. Scores of people felt some direct effect from that simple change in personnel. Some of them had only been in their positions as little as six weeks before being asked to make still another change in job assignment or location. When an administrative assistant asked me when all the changes would stop, I answered as honestly as I could, "Never. In fact, expect more changes to come even more rapidly in the future. *So get ready.*"

Change has both a domino and a ripple effect. A specific change might solve one problem, but then the solution often becomes the new problem or reveals several new problems. The root of the problem is not just the fact that the rate of change is gaining speed. The root of the problem is in our attitude toward the changes we cannot control.

Your organization must learn to become resilient to change and adapt to its changing environment or it will be doomed to ineffectiveness, irrelevance, and ultimately extinction. Just telling people to "buck up and get over it" is not enough. The most effective leaders are those who understand and use the principles of basic human patterns in response to change as they help the people they lead become more resilient and less resistant to change.[44] Building resilience to change will decrease the effects of OCSS and increase the effectiveness and productivity of the entire organization.

Leadership Hints

- Schedule times for discussion and dialogue to hear how people are feeling and processing change.

- Don't fall into the trap of defending the change. Instead let people process it.

<u>Followership Hints</u>
- One solitary life can make a difference.
- Take an attitude check. Is your negative response to the change related to your self-confidence, self-esteem, or self-concept?
- Decide to take a positive step toward being part of the solution and not part of the problem.

Attitude: The Life or Death of a Vision

"So we rebuilt the wall...for the people worked with all their heart." (Nehemiah 4:6)

Vision, Purpose, and Values Are Still Important

Every organization has some stated (or unstated) vision and purpose that describes the basic objective the organization wants to achieve. Regardless of how well the members of the organization might know and be able to recite the vision and purpose statements, this alone cannot guarantee that the organization will be successful in reaching its main objective. Success, as defined by the organization's vision and purpose, depends on all its members also sharing a set of core values and the belief that the vision can and will become reality as the organization fulfills its purpose. The degree to which each member understands and agrees with these three major pillars (vision, purpose, and values) will determine in large part how successful the organization can be at reaching its desired objective. Failure to lead the organization's members to share these same basic beliefs will doom the organization to mediocrity at best if it ever reaches any of its stated objectives. In successful organizations, the individual members form an interdependent relationship in which each one helps the organization to reach its objectives as the organization helps the members to reach their own.

Vision

The shared vision is the "What," the picture of the future the leadership of a company or team is trying to create. Many times the corporate vision is in reality a restatement of the leader's own personal vision. Everyone cannot be the visionary leader. Everyone can, however, have their own idea of what they want to accomplish, what they want to see become a reality in their own life. The corporate vision cannot be realized apart from individuals whose personal visions are in alignment with the corporate vision.

For the vision to be truly shared, it must be rooted in individual visions. By helping individuals to understand their own dreams and life goals, the organization can then help them to define what they want to accomplish in life and how working here can help them to do that.

Purpose

Purpose explains the "Why." "Why do we exist as an organization?" In carrying out the vision, the purpose helps clarify what unique contribution the organization is making to the world. Again, as the individuals who make up the organization understand their purpose in life, they have greater potential to contribute to the organization's purpose to the extent that these are in alignment. Unfortunately, many (perhaps most) people are just working for a paycheck. They need help defining their life purpose or mission.[45]

Rick Warren, in *The Purpose Driven Life*, states clearly that we can only find meaning for our lives as we recognize that we have been created with a purpose and that individual purpose "fits into a much larger, cosmic purpose that God has designed for eternity."[46] Warren also notes the need for community to fulfill our individual purposes. In effect, the organization has no purpose apart from the individual purposes of the people who form part of the organization. The individuals who make up the organization should have a sense that their contribution to the organization's purpose is also helping them to fulfill their personal purpose in life.

Values

Core values define how we ought to act. Shared core values help us to act in ways that are consistent with our mission (purpose) as we proceed toward realizing the vision.

Vision, purpose, and values together form the framework to answer the question "What do we believe in?" It is important to talk about the vision, purpose, and values at every level of the organization constantly. As people talk about the vision, it becomes increasingly clear, and enthusiasm grows as the vision becomes a shared vision. Individuals who seem fulfilled, satisfied, and enthusiastic about their jobs will most likely see how the organization is providing them an opportunity to contribute to something they already saw as important to them.

On the other hand, individuals who seem frustrated, unfulfilled and apathetic about their jobs probably have not been able to see how the organization's vision, purpose, and values complement their own. Rather than being forced to sacrifice one's personal vision for the larger cause, these individuals need help seeing how the two can be complementary. Diversity of views can be a source of strength as the vision is clarified. The key to keeping the diverse views from derailing the vision is in learning to assimilate those views that "harmonize" to enhance and enlarge the vision.

Two Needs - Seven Attitudes

Peter Senge described five general responses or attitudes toward the organization's vision: commitment, enrollment, compliance, noncompliance, or apathy. Compliance, however, can take one of three distinct forms, making a total of seven attitudes that individuals within the organization can demonstrate. [47]

Two Needs

While Senge accurately described the seven attitudes, he did not expand on why people react in these specific ways. This can best be understood by two areas of personal need people seek to satisfy in their employment: (1) *personal benefit* which includes salary, insurance, pension plans, position, recognition, or other non-tangible benefits (extrinsic values); and (2) a *personal sense of fulfillment* of their calling/vision (intrinsic values). The extent to which each individual will want to contribute to the organization's focus will depend on the degree to which they can see how both these needs are being fulfilled by their work within the company. This alignment will affect each individual's attitude and the degree to which they contribute effectively toward the company's goals or objectives.

Two Needs

© Larry Gay 2006, 2019

On the negative side, the degree to which an individual's need for personal benefit and/or personal sense of fulfillment are *not* met will also determine the degree to which the individual will become unproductive or even counterproductive to the organization's goals and objectives. Personal benefit and a personal sense of fulfillment will, in large part, determine the individual's attitude toward the company in general and the effectiveness of their work specifically. Different personalities place different values on these two needs.

Seven Attitudes

The following paragraphs and illustrations describe how the seven attitudes identified by Senge are affected by the individual's need for personal benefit and personal sense of fulfillment.

1. Committed

Only a few people are truly ***committed*** to the vision. These few want it and will do whatever they possibly can to make it happen. They live it, breathe it, and have such a desire to see it become reality that they say it is worth dying for.

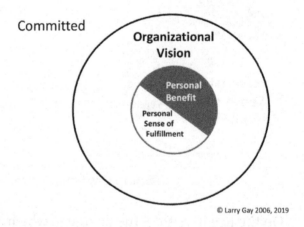

© Larry Gay 2006, 2019

These will include the founder or originator of the vision and a few people who join early on because they recognize in it something that they have already been longing to see before. No adaptation of their personal vision is necessary for them to find fulfillment in pursuit of the organizational vision. They might say, "I can't believe they pay me to do this!"

2. Enrolled

Another few will be ***enrolled***. These are the "early adopters" whose personal vision can easily fit within the organization's vision with little or no adaptation.

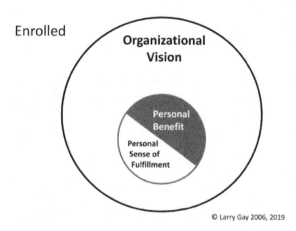

Enrolled

© Larry Gay 2006, 2019

Enrolled people will work within "the spirit of the law" to make the vision happen, but they might not feel the same level of ownership as those who are committed. They do not "live, eat, sleep, and breathe" the vision as the committed do. They do, however, truly desire to see the vision realized and will give their all to making it happen. Enrolled people believe in the vision as well as the way it is being implemented and feel they are in the right job within the organization to make a positive contribution.

3. Genuinely Compliant

The large majority of people in any organization most likely have an attitude of ***compliance***. There are several levels of compliance, some of which might appear very similar to enrollment and commitment. ***Genuine compliance*** might look like enrollment or commitment in that the genuinely compliant person sees the benefits of the vision and does everything expected and more. These "good soldiers" follow the letter of the law and are often tapped for leadership based on their above average performance. All or almost all of their personal vision can be realized in the context of the organization's vision. While the genuinely compliant can even quote the vision to the letter and they might even support the vision, they are not enrolled or committed to the point that they truly want the vision and would do whatever it might take to make the vision reality.

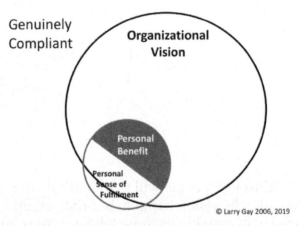

© Larry Gay 2006, 2019

Genuinely compliant people accept the vision and will work diligently for it, although they might not agree completely with the established strategy. In spite of any differences of opinion about the best ways to go about realizing the vision, they will do their best to follow and obey.

4. Formally Compliant

Another group demonstrates *formal compliance*. These are what Senge calls "pretty good soldiers." They do what is expected and no more.

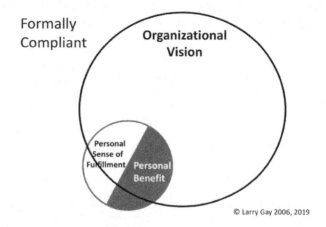

On the whole, formally compliant people see the benefits of the vision, but they do not take initiative to push the vision into reality. They can adapt to realize their personal vision, some of which may have to be achieved outside the organization or at a later time. They might support the vision to some degree, but they are primarily "going along" and not making waves. Much of their disagreement might be with methodology, structures, or how the vision is being implemented. Their sense of fulfillment is enough for them to stay, although they will certainly be open to "something better" if an offer comes their way.

5. Grudgingly Compliant

Some people will display a ***grudging compliance***. They will do what is expected because they feel obligated, but they do not see the real benefit and do not believe in the vision. Perhaps only to keep their jobs or because they see some other benefit outside the real vision, they do whatever is required of them but nothing more. At best, such compliance is more accurately described as passive-aggressive behavior. Grudgingly compliant people can be the most destructive force in the organization. They stay on and do enough to get by while letting it be known that they really are not on board. While they may not lead an open rebellion, they are, in effect, hoping that the direction the organization is taking will lead to failure.

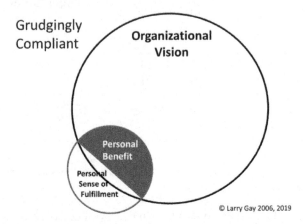

All or almost all of their personal sense of fulfillment is outside the organization's vision. In fact, they see the organization's vision as opposed to their personal vision. They blame the organization for their lack of productivity and inability to realize their personal vision.

Grudgingly compliant people put the greatest drag on leadership resources in the entire organization. These individuals do not see the value of the direction in which the organization is moving or are still opposed to changes that have taken place. Such people only remain with the organization because of the tangible benefits, such as medical or retirement, they receive from remaining with the organization. Grudgingly compliant people often do not realize how destructive they are to themselves and others.

6. Noncompliant

A certain number of people will be **noncompliant**. Their personal vision and the organizational vision are not aligned at all. Their attitude toward the vision is negative to the point of "I won't do it and you can't make me." Since they see no benefit in the vision, they may actively seek to undermine it or change it to a completely different direction.

© Larry Gay 2006, 2019

These people continue to drain resources from the organization, but they are completely outside the organizational vision and mission.

7. Apathetic

People in the last group demonstrate **apathy** for the vision. They are neither for it nor against it. They are simply along for the ride and waiting for the end of their shift or term. Like the noncompliant people, apathetic people are outside the circle of the organizational vision. These people only hang on because of the personal benefit they receive. They have no sense of fulfillment from their work.

© Larry Gay 2006, 2019

While they are not actively pulling against the direction of the vision, the apathetic employee is simply dead weight being dragged along without contributing significantly to the advancement of the organization to meet its objectives.

People in the organization will develop one of these seven attitudes (committed, enrolled, genuinely compliant, formally compliant, grudgingly compliant, noncompliant, or apathetic) as they respond to organizational change and their understanding of the organization's vision. As you consider these, you should be able to identify your own attitude as well as the attitudes of others around you. It is especially important to recognize the symptoms of noncompliance and grudging compliance since these represent the greatest challenge and threat to the realization of the vision.

Leadership Hints
- Are you a committed, enrolled, or compliant leader?
- How does your attitude affect your servant-stewardship as a leader?
- As you look at the people you lead, what attitudes do you think each of them demonstrates?

Followership Hints
- Time for another attitude check! Review the seven attitudes and try to identify which best describes your attitude toward your present organization and your current job assignment within it.
- If you continue in this attitude, will you contribute to the successful accomplishment of your personal life goals and also help the organization to reach its objectives?

All Aboard?
If we think of the organizational vision as a galley ship, imagine that the committed, enrolled, genuinely compliant,

and formally compliant people are all rowing together in sync and in the same direction. The grudgingly compliant are rowing in a haphazard manner, perhaps dragging their oars in resistance at times. Non-compliant people are rowing in the opposite direction or trying to take over the rudder. Finally, the apathetic personnel are hanging on outside the boat, or sitting on the edges dangling and dragging their feet in the water while everyone else rows.

© Larry Gay 2006, 2019

An organization that is made up primarily of genuinely and formally compliant people, with only a very few who are grudgingly compliant, can still be effective in reaching the vision. This requires, however, that the committed and enrolled leaders must spend a great deal of their time building an ethos within the organization as they help individuals see how moving to the next levels of alignment can help everyone to reach both the organization's objectives and their personal sense of purpose and accomplishment. A few grudgingly compliant people will actually see the light and make the change toward formal or even genuine compliance—hopefully, before the next big organizational change comes along!

If, however, there are significant numbers of grudgingly compliant people within the organization, productivity and effectiveness will definitely be a serious problem until their numbers are reduced, either by outplacement or they somehow finally see the light and are converted to at least formal compliance. Grudgingly compliant people often very carefully follow the rules to the letter of the law, but only enough to keep from being fired.

For the most part, noncompliant and apathetic people are eventually outplaced since their performance reviews will reveal their lack of contribution to the organization's stated objectives. Supervisors, however, often delay too long in confronting people who have demonstrated their opposition to the vision. While we always hope to bring people along and we should give them time to adjust to major changes, we also must recognize when it is time to admit that an employee just is not working out. (See the chapter on "Confronting for Change.")

"One of Us Needs Some Relief"

Frustration levels go up while productivity goes down as the people who work closest with the grudgingly compliant, noncompliant, and apathetic approach the point of desperation. They might feel like comedian Jerry Clower's friend, John Eubanks, who climbed up a tree to try and knock a raccoon out of its nest to be shot by his friends on the ground. The "raccoon" turned out to be a lynx which put up a great fight for his life. In the heat of the clawing, gnashing, and screaming, John finally yelled down to his friends, "Shoot this thing!" His friends were reluctant, for fear they might hit John instead of the big wild cat. In desperation, John yelled down, "Just shoot up here amongst us! One of us has got to have some relief!"

Supervisors need to recognize how they are hurting the organization by delaying the needed confrontation. Often, very good people end up leaving because they can no longer tolerate the poisonous attitudes of the noncompliant and grudgingly compliant people, and they have no reserve energies to continue carrying the dead weight of the apathetic. In their case, the shot from Jerry's rifle brings down the wrong target.

Can We Settle for Compliance?

Leaders sometimes make the mistake of trying to get all their personnel to become enrolled or committed to the vision. Sometimes, supervisors might even try to sell people on the benefits of the vision when they are not fully enrolled or committed but are themselves operating out of a formal or genuine compliance. At times, Senge suggested, managers need to be satisfied with compliance. People must be allowed to choose to enroll or commit. Either they can see the benefits of the vision, or they can't. No amount of selling can convince them of the benefits if they can't see it.

They can, however, be brought along from compliance to enrollment by allowing them to feel a sense of safety as they are allowed to see how their personal visions can be realized in the context of the organization's vision. This is best done in one-on-one performance reviews where a supervisor can spend time listening to understand the individual's life goals and purpose.

As the supervisor understands the individual's personal goals and desires, they can find points of connection with the organization's vision. This becomes the ground on which critical communication takes place to begin moving from the present reality to the future vision as individuals see how working within this organization can help them achieve their personal sense of fulfillment.

The degree to which these three circles coincide or overlap will determine how much effort is required to share the vision and help people get on board as they begin to understand what the vision is and how it can be realized with their help.

You Don't Need a Carrot or a Stick

Some leaders might be surprised to discover that, even years after the major changes have taken place, there are still a significant number of people in the grudging compliance category. The question becomes, "How can we help grudgingly compliant people move to formal or even genuine compliance?" The answer is in first identifying where their personal vision coincides with the organization's vision and then rewarding even baby steps in the right direction as they attempt to "get on board."

Some leaders at various levels in the organization are themselves only formally compliant and therefore do not fully understand how to bring other people along in any way other than to repeat what they interpret as "orders" coming from above. Since they are not in total agreement with some of the direction of the organization, they might find it difficult to advocate parts of the vision positively to people they supervise. Although formally compliant leaders can help people to see the value in complying, as they have complied, it will be difficult for them to lead people to go beyond their own level of compliance unless the individuals already had a personal commitment to a vision similar to that of the organization.

I was asked once in an interview if I preferred to use the carrot or the stick in my leadership style. I responded, "Neither." Negative behaviors require corrective action and positive behaviors deserve appropriate rewards. This, however, is not the same as the "carrot or stick" approach. Self-motivated people are far more productive than people who are forced, manipulated, or coerced into compliance.

People generally do not respond positively to negative stimuli. They are much more likely to respond positively to *positive* stimuli, even small rewards for small advances. Leaders need to identify specific points of disagreement as the resistant people see them. An individual might be opposed to the methodology being applied and still be in complete agreement with the stated vision, purpose, and values of the organization. Or the disagreement might be related to specific policies and practices rather than the strategic direction outlined by the vision and purpose. Leaders can help some people adapt to the current direction simply by giving them the opportunity to express their concerns in a non-threatening environment. In some cases, an innovative "third alternative" might surface that could never have emerged outside the context of open communication.

The key here is to find what motivates each individual within the organization and then connect one-on-one with their motivations. This requires leaders at every level learning to *serve* the people they lead. You can then help them see how working within the organization in its new direction can help each person to accomplish more of what they want to accomplish with their lives.

Leadership Hints

- How does your own attitude toward organizational changes affect the way you serve and lead others?
- How can you better serve the people you lead to help them make adjustments in their alignment with the vision and purpose of your organization?
- Will your answers to either of the questions above require an adjustment of your own attitude or movement toward the next level of compliance, enrollment, or commitment?

Followership Hints

- What is keeping you from being your most effective and productive self in your job?
- What can you reasonably change to make things better?
- Are you willing to do what is necessary to get better aligned with your organization's direction? If not, what alternatives do you see and are you willing to act on these?

Stress and Job Dissatisfaction

One ship sails East,
And another West,
By the self-same winds that blow,
'Tis the set of the sails
And not the gales,
That tells the way we go.[48]

Jordan and Kim both work for the same organization, in the same job, with the same title, the same boss, and they receive exactly the same pay. Jordan loves this job and has very few complaints about the way things are going. Kim, on the other hand, is growing increasingly dissatisfied with the direction the organization is taking and seems to complain about everything. Kim is so stressed by it all that burnout is just around the corner.

After talking with Jordan and Kim you might ask, "Are these two really working at the same job in the same place with the same boss?" How can one person love what the organization is doing and be thrilled with the job while the other person is convinced the whole organization is going down the drain? What makes the difference?

You Always Have Choices

Although commitment to or compliance with the vision is not an antidote to stress, the degree to which the individual is satisfied in their position or assignment within the organization will depend, in large part, on the degree to which the individual feels a sense of fulfillment in the job. Individuals who feel their sense of purpose or personal calling is being limited by the organization's belief system (vision, purpose, and values) will be in a perpetual state of distress that will manifest itself in behaviors that work against the organization's objectives.

Some members of the organization can honestly say they are "on board" with the vision, purpose, and core values of the organization although their actions may become counterproductive to that vision and purpose. If they do not share the same basic beliefs related to the direction in which the organization is moving, the methodologies being employed, the structures that are in place or perhaps even the way changes are being communicated, then they might not yet really be "on board" with the changes.

When we are faced with the stress of organizational change, we basically have three choices: (1) stay and be satisfied, (2) stay and be a problem, or (3) leave. The option we choose is largely determined by our sense of satisfaction and fulfillment in the job. Like adding weights in a balance, the decision to stay is based on the weight of positive influences contributing to job satisfaction as opposed to the negative stressors that cause dissatisfaction. William Byham called these "Zapps!" and "Sapps."[49] The chart below lists some of the major factors that contribute to a person's satisfaction or dissatisfaction with their job.

Factors Contributing to Job Satisfaction	Stressors Contributing to Dissatisfaction
(+) Alignment between personal and organizational vision, purpose, values (+) Sense of fulfillment in line with one's giftedness and strengths (+) Good Relationships (+) Appreciation (+) Benefits (+) "Zapps!" (Encouraging words that build up) (+) Helpful Policies (+) Empowerment	(-) Misalignment between personal and organizational vision, purpose, values (-) Working outside one's giftedness or strengths (-) Strained relationships (-) Busy work (-) Devaluation (-) "Sapps!" (Discouraging words, criticism that tears down) (-) Rules and regulations that restrict (-) Micro-management
Outcome = Stay and be satisfied	Outcome = Stay and be dissatisfied, unproductive, become a problem, or leave

We would like to believe that everyone in the organization is genuinely seeking to be true to their personal vision or sense of calling. For some people, that factor will carry so much weight that it counterbalances all the negative stressors. Other people, however, will come to the point that the only positive factor contributing to their job satisfaction is the personal benefits they receive (including, but not limited to, monetary benefits).

When the balance tilts to the dissatisfaction side, stress mounts up and can cloud or color the decision-making processes. The longer a person stays in a state of dissatisfaction, the more stress will grow and the more difficult it will be for them to reset their sails—either to realign themselves with the new direction of the organization, or to find a place in another organization that is going their way.

'Tis the Set of the Sails

Grudgingly compliant, noncompliant, and apathetic members will exhibit greater levels of stress and job dissatisfaction than will their colleagues who are formally compliant, genuinely compliant, enrolled, or committed to the vision. Because their sails are set for a different direction, these individuals will feel that the fulfillment of their purpose or calling is being limited by the demands placed on them by the organization. They will be in a perpetual state of distress that will manifest itself in behaviors that work against the organization's objectives. In the end, they will be unlikely to reach their personal goals as well.

Leadership Hints

- What is your assessment of the general morale among the people you lead?
- Look back over the list of factors contributing to job dissatisfaction. If a number of people seem dissatisfied, what common factors can you identify that contribute to the dissatisfaction and stress?
- What positive actions come to mind that you could take to help people better align with your organization's vision, purpose, and values?
- Are you willing to take action?

Followership Hints

- How is your sail set?
- As you look back over the list of factors contributing to job satisfaction or dissatisfaction, which way is your balance tilting?
- What steps can you take to improve your own job satisfaction?
- Do you feel your current job allows you to work from your giftedness and strengths a majority of the time?
- Is there anything you can do to help a co-worker feel more satisfied and fulfilled in their job?
- So, what do you intend to do?

When Enough Is Enough

> *"Failure to deal with the problems people and organizations face can be the most unloving action of all."* (Leith Anderson) [50]

> *"Warn a divisive person once, and then warn him a second time. After that, have nothing to do with him. You may be sure that such a man is warped and sinful; he is self-condemned."* (Titus 3:10-11)

For many supervisors the most difficult part of leadership is confronting someone whose behavior or performance is unacceptable. Remember, the purpose of corrective action is *not* to punish the individual for poor behavior or poor performance. It is your responsibility as a leader to help people understand the vision and adjust their behaviors to align with it to the degree that they can.

A noncompliant person should be made aware of the consequences of continued failure to meet expectations. Even if the individual becomes grudgingly compliant, there comes a point where such passive-aggressive behavior becomes destructive and unacceptable. It's one thing for a person to use their influence to effect change that might help the organization fulfill its mission. It's something else entirely, however, when the complaints become destructive and contrary to the direction established by the organization's leadership.

(See more on corrective action in the chapter on "Confronting for Change".

The Most Unloving Action of All

Outplacement is often seen as a heartless action. The real heartless action, however, is when an unacceptable behavior is allowed to go unchecked until things have gotten unbearable for others working close to the offending individual. That would be like a father "correcting" his young child who is misbehaving by saying, "I'm only going to warn you about this 17 more times and then I'm really going to do something about it!" Of course, the child will go on being obnoxious and unruly, disturbing everyone else within sight or sound until the father finally takes drastic action. If he had gently and firmly corrected the child earlier, he could have avoided a lot of discomfort for everyone, including the child.

Failure to take administrative action hurts both the offending individual and the whole organization. Grudgingly compliant people can be like a cancer growing in the organization. The longer you delay in taking the inevitable, definitive action, the more you allow the cancer to grow. Long-growing cancers require more extensive surgery and more serious post-operative treatment. In the same way, if corrective actions have not helped the individual to make the necessary attitudinal change in a reasonable (and clearly stated) time frame, then the longer you postpone taking action, the more difficult it will be for all concerned.

On the Right Train, in the Right Car and in the Right Seat

Sometimes the destructive attitude is the result of the individual being in a position where they feel the job is not a good match for their gifts and strengths. In such cases, it might be possible to tweak a job description or help the individual find another place of service where they can find satisfaction and fulfillment within the organization. That can be wonderful—as long as you are not just transferring your problems to another department!

If the individual continues in grudging compliance and demonstrates no willingness to change to a more positive attitude, then the most loving action a leader can take is to coach the person to realize that their personal vision does not align with that of the organization. In those cases, you can guide them to recognize that the fulfillment of their personal vision can only be achieved in another setting that aligns with their goals.

Leading the person to understand that they can better fulfill their sense of purpose in another setting is like helping them find their seat in the right car on the right train going in the right direction to get where they want to go. By confronting these individuals with gentleness and respect, you have the opportunity to challenge them to reach their maximum potentiality and productivity while also maximizing your organization's resources to realize its vision.

Leadership Hints

- Don't make the mistake of ignoring the problem and hoping it will go away on its own.
- Also, don't make the mistake of jumping to the conclusion that just firing someone will make everything all better.
- Talk with people about the source of their dissatisfaction. Seek first to understand, then to be understood. Make every effort to help them grow to an acceptable level of compliance.
- Describe for yourself what the change in behavior will look like, when the change must be made, and how you will know steps are being taken toward the change. Then communicate these very clearly and positively to the individual, both verbally and in writing.
- Don't make threats. Do keep your word; follow through on corrective actions. (See the chapter on "Confronting for Change" for more on administering corrective action.)

Followership Hints

- You really do have a choice.
- Take responsibility for your own attitude and actions.
- Remember, negative attitudes and actions usually do not produce positive reactions. If you have tried to offer positive suggestions of ways to make things

better and they have been rejected or ignored, remember that you still have choices.

> **Servant-stewards build a culture of people who are not obsessed by the law or policies but who see the practicality of principles which underlie the law.**
> - Their priority is not on policies, but rather on the proclamation of the gospel. (1 Tim. 1:8-10; 2 Tim. 2:3-13; Titus 2:1-14; 3:1-9)

The Stewardship Factor

"It is required of stewards that one be found trustworthy." (1 Cor. 4:2)

During major organizational changes, we spend a lot of time and energy trying to "bring people along," help them to "get on board," or "buy into the vision." We might even talk about wanting everyone to "own" the vision. While such efforts might be well-intentioned, they might also be expending unnecessary energy toward an unreachable goal. In fact, no one really "owns" the organization's vision. We are not owners of the vision; we are merely **stewards**.

For the organizational vision to be realized, leaders must recognize their stewardship responsibilities. The most effective leaders are good stewards of both the vision *and* the people they lead. Leaders who exhibit an attitude of stewardship can make a significant difference in the general attitude or morale of the people they lead.

We have a pronoun problem.

Consider the difference between two types of leaders. At least twice in my career I have worked with supervisors/leaders who personalized everything: my team, my staff, my people, my project—my, my, my! Each of these leaders was insecure and felt threatened by anyone who took any personal initiative beyond the bounds of their specific written job descriptions. When any subordinate received any word of praise from a constituent, they would take such a compliment to be a threat to them as if someone were going to take away their position of authority. Each of these supervisors eventually had some serious crises in their leadership because of their insecurities and inability to let go of things that really were not theirs to hold on to.

I also have had the privilege of working with some very excellent and effective leaders in my career. These leaders did not feel threatened when they heard someone compliment a subordinate. In fact, they expressed joy and appreciation for such comments. On one occasion, early in my career, my supervisor called me into his office and asked me to close the door. I could not imagine what I had done to deserve a reprimand and I could think of no other reason for him to call me in. "I just received a phone call about you," he said. "It was a constituent telling me what a good job they thought you were doing." He went on to say he considered a compliment to anyone on his team to be a compliment to the whole team, so he felt complimented too! "And by the way," he ended, "keep up the good work!"

You can imagine which of these inspired me to contribute more effectively to the organization for which I worked.

Effective leaders who are good stewards learn to talk more in the first person plural and less in the first personal singular. They use a lot more "we," "our," and "ours" and lot less "I," "my," and "mine." Such a stewardship attitude builds loyalty and commitment. It inspires people to more effective followership. And effective followership is a requirement for effective leadership.

Effective stewards also avoid talking about "they," "their", or "them" when communicating vision, direction, policies, or principles. Even though stewards are not owners, they do have an obligation to represent the interests of the owner. Stewards are regarded as trustworthy to act on behalf of the owner with all the authority of the owner. Regardless of whether the steward has actively participated in the formulation of policy, procedure, or direction, they will communicate with confidence what **we** must do to reach **our** goals in pursuit of **our** vision. (I suppose that starts to sound like taking ownership, doesn't it?)

Stewards of the Vision

For the organizational vision to be realized, leaders must recognize the stewardship principle. Stewards are not owners. As a stewards of the larger organizational vision, we all give up possession of our own personal visions in order for them to become reality.

The organization can realize its vision only to the extent that individuals connect and contribute to the corporate vision with their personal visions. Leaders should help the people they lead to see that their own personal vision is part of something larger. The closer the alignment between individuals' personal sense of fulfillment with the organization's vision, the more they will believe in what the organization is trying to accomplish. The more they believe in it, the harder they will work to make it succeed.

The truth of the matter is, your organization *cannot* reach its maximum potential without every member's participation. Being honest with personnel to say "we need your support to reach this vision," can go a long way toward gaining *followership* once the leaders have demonstrated their own personal trustworthiness as good stewards.

Leadership Hints

It is appropriate to use the first person singular when you are taking responsibility for an action (e.g., "I made that decision"). Otherwise, and especially when giving credit, use the plural (e.g., "Our team did a great job!")

Evaluate how you use inclusive language and how your form of communication conveys your underlying values.

Help your followers evaluate how their personal vision and values are realized through meeting the organizational vision and values. This can be done as a part of regular performance evaluations in a formal way and also affirmed in ongoing conversations when you "catch" the person succeeding at something that fits with both their personal vision and organizational vision.

Followership Hints

Followers are stewards, too. While you might not feel you have influence over the entire organization, you have been given some measure of responsibility for a portion of the organization's success. You are a steward of that portion, so take responsibility for it!

(Copies of this chapter are available as a separate article by writing us at LEAD360@gmail.com or visit our website: www.LEAD360.com.)

Resolving for Harmony
Principles for Dealing with Conflict

*"Man must evolve for all human conflict a method
which rejects revenge, aggression and retaliation. The
foundation of such a method is love."*
(Martin Luther King, Jr.)

*"...Speaking the truth in love,
we are to grow up in every way
into him who is the head, into Christ."*
(Ephesians 4:15)

*"Blessed are the peacemakers,
for they shall be called the children of God."*
(Matthew 5:9)

**Servant-stewards know how to deal
appropriately with conflicts. (1 Tim. 1:3-4)**

Caring Enough to Confront – Care-Fronting

When it comes to conflict and confrontation, many
leaders make one of two mistakes. Either they act as if the
problem will go away if they ignored it long enough or they
wait until the problem develops into such a conflictive
situation that they explode in self-defense and destructive
anger that can ultimately result in fatal damage to the
relationship with the other individual.

Conflict situations are those in which the concerns of
two people appear to be incompatible. In his classic book,
Caring Enough to Confront, David Augsburger stated, "It is

not the conflicts that need to concern us, but how the conflicts are handled."[51] Conflict, he asserted, is always with us and is neither good nor bad, right nor wrong. The problem arises when individuals deal inappropriately with conflict. Augsburger coined the word "care-fronting" as a way to deal with conflict in an appropriately loving yet firm way. Caring communicates the desire to maintain respectful relationships while confronting lets the other individual know one's feelings, needs, values, and desires. (Refer also to the chapter on "Confronting for Change.")

Family of Origin Issues

The way you handle conflict is likely influenced by the way conflict was handled in your family growing up. Take a few minutes to reflect on the following questions:

1. How did your parents handle conflict both with each other and with you?

2. How did your parents teach you to handle conflict with siblings or friends?

3. How do you usually handle conflict?

4. Is this similar to your parents' usual method of handling conflict?

5. Do you think your usual method of handling conflict is more indicative of how your family handled conflict or more indicative of your own personal style?

6. How does the culture of your work environment influence your approach to handling conflict?

7. Are you satisfied with your approach to handling conflict? Why or why not?

Assess Your Preferred Style

If you have not already completed a conflict mode assessment, now would be a good time to pause and take the Style Matters questionnaire.[52] It only takes 15 minutes online and will provide a wealth of information to help you consider how you tend to approach conflict in the "calm" (when there is a simple difference of opinion) and how you might shift to another style in the "storm" (when it becomes a full-blown conflict).

All conflict mode instruments identify five styles of dealing with conflict. Although the terminology varies slightly, the five possibilities are plotted on a Mouton-Blake Grid with one axis measuring how much the individual values the task or issue at hand and the other axis measuring how much value is given to the relationship.

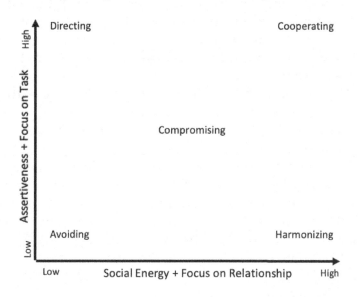

1. *Directing* or Competing = high task, low relationship ("I win, you lose.")
2. *Avoiding* = low task, low relationship (lose/lose, "I'll just leave.")
3. *Harmonizing* or Complying = low task, high relationship ("I lose, you win.")
4. *Compromising* = in the middle ("We both win a little and lose a little.")
5. *Cooperating* or Collaborating = high task, high relationship ("We both win.")

The Birkman Components of Assertiveness and Social Energy add another dimension to the two axes.

Assertiveness has to do with the tendency to speak up and express opinions forcefully. A high value on task along with higher Assertiveness will make you more likely to speak up and assert your opinion in conflict (Directing). When high Assertiveness becomes negative under stress, it becomes aggressiveness. Those with lower Assertiveness scores will prefer to be more suggestive rather than directive. Low assertiveness becomes passive under stress.

Social Energy has to do with a preference for group and team participation (on the high end of the scale) or working independently (on the low end). The more you value the relationship, the more likely you are to want others to be in harmony (Harmonizing).

The person with high Social Energy combined with high Assertiveness will be willing to spend the time and energy necessary to come to an agreement that satisfies everyone in the group (Cooperating).

Under stress, the person with high Social Energy and high Assertiveness can spend too much time talking, trying to convince everyone to come to an agreement. A person with high Social Energy and low Assertiveness might become overly swayed by the group and not speak up. Low Social Energy and low Assertiveness can lead the person to avoid the conflict completely and even withdraw from the people involved (Avoiding).

Choose Your Style Carefully – A Time for Every Style

Since *avoiding* is low on task and low on relationship, nothing is accomplished by not confronting. *Avoiding* is unproductive if the issue is never resolved. This style is low on task and low on relationship—I lose, you lose, we all lose. If you feel you are in a position of lower power, you are likely to avoid bringing up the issue. Sometimes, however, it can be wise to avoid dealing with the conflict until a more appropriate time or until emotions have cooled down. (Example: "Can we talk about this tomorrow morning after staff meeting?")

At other times, the issue really is not important enough to warrant spending the time and energy needed. For the sake of the relationship, *harmonizing* might be the best choice—You win, I lose. (Example: "I'm really fine with whatever you want to do. You choose and I will be happy with it.") Don't default to a harmonizing style if you really do have a desire or opinion about the outcome.

When the task is of utmost importance, *directing* or *competing* can be the right style to use. In a crisis or life-threatening emergency, you want someone to take charge and use the command mode effectively. Of course, emergencies are not the only times with directing is appropriate. The purpose here is not to build relationship because the task is of such importance—I win, you lose. (Example: "I need that report completed by tomorrow afternoon so I will have time to look over it before the board meeting on Thursday.") When misused or over-used, this command style of directing or competing can be an impediment to building relationships in the team, so use it carefully.

Compromise is sometimes seen as the style of last resort. It involves both give and take—I win some, you win some; I lose some, you lose some. (Example: "I'll agree to take over Pat's accounts if you will postpone launching the new project until after the first of the year.")

Collaborating or *cooperating* requires the most time and energy. When both the task and the relationship are of high importance, the investment can be worthwhile. Save this style for larger issues that can also build or preserve unity as they are resolved. It requires more time because together both sides are working to discover a "third option" that neither party alone would have imagined. This is the win/win style. (Example: "Come, let's reason together. Let's get all the issues out on the table and see if we can think a new thought.")

Although your personality influences your preferred style of dealing with conflict, if you allow yourself to become overly dependent on any one style, you will limit your effectiveness. The most effective leaders learn to use each of the five styles according to the need of the specific situation or circumstance. Every decision in every situation does not have equal importance. The ability to respond in varied ways and the flexibility to match your response to the way the conflict is developing can become invaluable tools in your supervisory toolkit.

The object is to respond genuinely and appropriately with both love and power in balance as you develop a care-fronting relationship. *"For God gave us a spirit not of fear but of power and love and self-control."* (2 Tim. 1:7)

Use the following chart to determine the best style for the specific situation.

Directing (Competing) High Assertiveness/Low Social Energy
Useful when a commander is needed. Can limit the growth of others.

Use it when:	Skills needed:
• Quick action must be taken • Unpopular decisions must be made • Vital issues must be handled • Protecting self-interests	• Arguing or debating • Using rank or influence • Asserting your opinions and feelings • Standing your ground • Stating your position clearly

Avoiding Low Assertiveness/Low Social Energy
Often used out of fear of conflict or lack of confidence in conflict management skills.

Use it when:	Skills needed:
• Issues are of low importance • You need to reduce tensions • You need to buy some time • You are in a position of lower power	• Ability to withdraw • Ability to sidestep issues • Ability to leave things unresolved • Sense of timing

Harmonizing (Accommodating) Low Assertiveness/High Social Energy
Can be problematic when one uses the mode to "keep a tally" or to be a martyr without communicating desired reciprocation.

Use it when:	Skills needed:
• Showing reasonableness • Developing performance • Creating good will • Keeping peace • Issue or outcome is of low importance to you	• Forgetting your desires • Selflessness • Ability to yield to others • Obeying orders

Compromising Moderate Assertiveness/Moderate Social Energy
Some people define compromise as "giving up more than you want," while others see compromise as both parties winning.

Use it when:	Skills needed:
• Dealing with issues of moderate importance • You have equal power status • You have a strong commitment for resolution	• Negotiating • Finding a middle ground • Assessing value • Making concessions

Cooperating (Collaborating) High Assertiveness/High Social Energy
Described as "putting an idea on top of an idea on top of an idea...in order to achieve the best solution to a conflict." A creative solution to the conflict that would not have been generated by a single individual. Some would say it is always the best mode to use, but it takes a great deal of time and energy.

Use it when:	Skills needed:
• It is important to the people who are constructing an integrative solution • Issues are too important to compromise • Merging perspectives • Gaining commitment • Improving relationships • Learning	• Active listening • Non-threatening confrontation • Identifying concerns • Analyzing input

The Secret to Unity and Harmony

Unity is vitally important for any team to be effective. Conflict disturbs unity. Perhaps for this reason, Jesus prayed for our unity on the night before his crucifixion. He asked that his disciples, as well as those who would follow later, would be one even as he and his Father are one. (Jn. 17:20-22) The secret to maintaining unity in the body is love. For some reason, Jesus *commanded* us to love one another and he *prayed* for our unity—not the other way around. He commanded his disciples that they were to love one another as he had loved them. Indeed, the obvious display of love among the disciples would be the distinctive mark by which others would know that they were/are his disciples. (Jn. 13:34-35)

Deliberate, focused love is the ultimate weapon for dealing with conflict: love for God, love for oneself, love for other believers, and love for unbelievers. Such love demands that we deal with conflict and not avoid it. As Leith Anderson says, "The most unloving action of all can be to ignore the problems that people and organizations face."[53]

First Corinthians 12, 13, and 14 provide clear instructions for dealing with difficult issues in the body of believers. The three chapters must be taken together to fully understand the principles in the passage.

Chapter 12 focuses on the unity of the body (unity *not* uniformity). Diversity in the body contributes to and is essential for its unity. This is the unity Jesus prayed for the night before his crucifixion. (Jn. 17:20-22) Chapter 13 focuses on love because love is the glue that holds the body together in unity. Jesus did not suggest; he *commanded* his followers to love one another. (Jn. 13:32-33) Finally, chapter 14 indicates that, if the body is bound together in unity by love, then the body can deal with critical issues. Although the specific passage refers to the issue of speaking in tongues, the principle is the same regardless of what the critical issue might be. Peace can only be achieved in the body through active love.

Blessed are the Peacemakers

"Blessed are the peacemakers, for they shall be called the children of God." (Mt. 5:9)

At 7:19 am on September 19, 1985, a violent earthquake hit Mexico City followed by a second quake just 36 hours later. As many as 20,000 people were killed, thousands of buildings were destroyed or severely damaged, and more than 100,000 people were left homeless. The term for disaster victim in Spanish is *damnificado,* which is different from being the victim of a personal assault (*victima*) and more accurately describes how the displaced victims felt. Within hours of the initial quake, volunteers began mobilizing, both from within Mexico and from neighboring countries, particularly the USA. The second big quake that hit the following evening was so destructive that the president of Mexico issued an unprecedented call for international help.

We were living in Mexico City at the time and I was thrust into the role of disaster relief coordinator for Southern Baptist representatives in Mexico City. Baptist Men's groups from Texas, Oklahoma, Mississippi, and Louisiana responded and set up feeding stations in four central locations under the authority of the federal and municipal governments of Mexico. For almost four weeks volunteers from the USA and Mexico manned the four field kitchens that fed over 25,000 people each day while the government prepared longer term shelters that would house families for over a year until they could be relocated to permanent housing. Before the USA volunteers left, they helped design and construct army style field kitchens in four of these "permanent shelters."

The Baptist Convention of Mexico agreed to provide a full-time coordinator for each of these long-term shelters. Each coordinator would work under the authority of a general director named by the government to train and coordinate teams of shelter residents who would take turns working with volunteers from local churches to prepare meals from the supplies that were being provided through the government. Little by little we withdrew all outside volunteers except the four coordinators who continued to organize the shelter residents to take turns working in the kitchens. For a while, I would visit each shelter weekly to encourage the kitchen coordinators and the shelter directors employed by the government. By the end of the first year, I was visiting each shelter only about once a month. At that point, we felt the kitchens should be operating on their own and really did not require the presence of the outside coordinators. So I visited with each of the four directors privately and shared that we would be withdrawing our personnel from their positions.

In each case, each of the four directors looked at me with tears in his eyes and said almost the exact same words: "Please do not take your coordinator from us."

"Why? I asked. You already have well trained people in the shelter who can continue to do the work without an outside coordinator."

I especially remember the first director I spoke with that day and how he explained, "Yes, but here is the thing. You have said that your coordinator must take one day off each week away from the shelter."

"That's right," I responded. "He would be no good to you if he burned out from neglecting the need for Sabbath rest. God was pretty smart when he commanded us to do that. So what is your point?"

"The point is really simple. When your coordinator is here there is peace and harmony. The ladies all work together without any major arguments or conflicts. But on the day when the coordinator is not here, the kitchen seems to fall apart. It does not matter who is there, they just don't seem to be able to work together. The coordinator doesn't have to do anything except just be here and his simple presence makes a difference between peace and chaos."

"How interesting." I said. "You know, Jesus commented on that when he said, 'Blessed are the peacemakers for they shall be called the children of God.'"

"Yes! That's it!" he exclaimed. "He is a child of God and he is the peacemaker. Please don't take away our peacemaker."

Peacemaking is More than the Absence of Conflict

The goal of conflict resolution is peacemaking—the restoration of relationships. Ken Sande proposed in his book, *The Peacemaker*, "When Christians learn to be peacemakers, they can turn conflict into an opportunity to strengthen relationships, preserve valuable resources, and make their lives a testimony to the love and power of Christ."[54]

Sande framed the goal of peacemaking as maintaining or reestablishing *Shalom*, the peace that God loves. "Peacemaking is not an optional activity for a believer. . . God wants you to strive earnestly, diligently, and continually to maintain harmonious relationships with those around you."[55] *Shalom* is more than simple peace, it is the norm that God intends for his creation by design and for redemption. Sin disrupts *Shalom* and causes destructive conflict.

Cornelius Plantinga agreed. *Shalom*, he said, is the way things are supposed to be. When things are not the way they are supposed to be, then *Shalom* is broken and that is sin.[56]

To effectively maintain *Shalom* requires trusting in the sovereignty of God that he will do everything he knows is good while also recognizing the roles that Satan and people play in conflicts. It also means trusting in the leadership He has chosen. Trust is a decision we make. We can decide to trust in the sovereignty of God and obey him, even when times are tough. We can also decide to trust the other person, even when we are not absolutely certain of their trustworthiness.

Peacemaking that is rooted in the sovereignty of God and trusting in the leadership He has chosen, can lead to *shalom* in a person's very demeanor. That *shalom* overflows into an attitude and presence that brings peace to the environment in which that person exists.

Solving Problems Before They Become Conflicts

In his short book, *Solving Problems Before They Become Conflicts,* Norm Wakefield defined conflict as a mismanaged problem. "Conflict arises when we neglect problem solving, or we use ineffective problem-solving procedures."[57] Wakefield pointed out the unfortunate reality that few individuals have been carefully trained to be skilled problem solvers, leaving most persons in the predicament of trying to deal with problems without having the proper skills to do so.

Wakefield distinguished differences between problem solving and conflict. In problem solving both individuals apply their energy to seeking a common solution. In conflict each individual's energy is aimed at advocating for their own solution. Problem solving, he insisted, keeps the problem as the focus while conflict focuses on the self.

Personality and Problem-Solving

Interpersonal problems or personality conflicts have three underlying factors at work: perception, emotion, and communication. Perception is your way of interpreting the facts from your unique vantage point. "Differences are defined by the difference between your thinking and theirs.... Facts, even if established, may do nothing to solve the problem."[58] The Birkman Method highlights differences in perception related to personality differences. As a B-17 bomber pilot and instructor in World War II, Roger Birkman noticed how individual differences in visual and interpersonal perceptions had a visible impact on pilot performance and learning. He began a life-long study of human behavior that resulted in The Birkman Method®. Dr. Birkman said, "The reality of life is that your perceptions—right or wrong—influence everything you do. When you get a proper perspective of your perceptions, you may be surprised how many other things fall into place." Effective problem solving requires understanding the problem from the other person's perspective.

Emotions must be considered because "feelings may be more important than talk."[59] Emotions often communicate more deeply than words. Wakefield also noted the influence that emotions have on unresolved problems becoming conflicts. "Emotions impact problem solving because *we communicate by emotions,* as well as by thoughts (cognitively)."[60]

Some people are more emotionally expressive and want to engage others in conversations that include how they feel in a situation. This is what Birkman calls high Emotional Energy. Individuals with low Emotional Energy focus on the practical side and are able to separate emotion from the facts. They might describe themselves as being objective, focused on results, and working toward an immediate solution. They are able to separate issues from emotions in their conversation. While they do have emotions, they are able to deal with them separately and probably privately.

It's important to remember, however, that most (though not all) people do not want to be treated the same way they treat others. Most people who are very matter of fact in their speech really want you to be more considerate of how they feel about it as you are addressing them. Conversely, sometimes the person who is expressing a lot of emotion in their conversation really wants you to be more focused on the facts and tell them like it is.

Communication presents the biggest challenge in negotiation. Often, each side is trying so hard to make the other side see the problem from their point of view that they cannot effectively listen. As the unresolved problem becomes a conflict, communication breaks down even further. The two sides ultimately give up on each other and no longer even attempt any serious communication. Instead of talking *to* each other, they talk *at* each other or *about* each other—primarily to impress third parties.

The root concern related to conflict, according to Wakefield, is not the problems individuals face, but *the individuals themselves.*[61] The fact that people have different personalities means they approach problems in different ways and that can result in conflict. Wakefield illustrated this point by relating the biblical example of the three different ways Nabal, David, and Abigail all approached the problem when David requested security payment from Nabal as recorded in 1 Samuel 25.

Nabal was described as a "very rich man." David and his marauders had been camped in the vicinity of Nabal's large herds of sheep and goats. When the time for shearing came, David sent word to Nabal, pointing out that nothing had gone missing while they were there and asking for provisions for his men in return for having acted civilly and provided protection to Nabal's shepherds. They were coming at a feast time when a number of animals would have been slaughtered to feed all the servants and others would likely have been invited as well.

Although there would have been plenty to share and he could easily afford it, Nabal responded with arrogance and contempt, refusing hospitality to David and his men. David's reaction was one of heated anger as he organized his men to attack and wipe out Nabal's entire company in return for Nabal's lack of gratitude for the service he and his men had performed.

Meanwhile, an astute servant reported the incident to Abigail, Nabal's wife, and urged her to take action to avert the impending disaster. There was already plenty of food prepared, more than enough to feed David's six hundred men. So, she quickly ordered her servants to load up the pack animals and she delivered the provision to David in person with her elaborate apologies for her husband's despicable behavior and an appeal to David's good graces. David responded graciously and the only blood spilt that day was from lambs and goats.

Abigail demonstrated skill at keeping a problem from becoming a conflict by: listening to wise counsel (of her servant), acting with intelligence, initiating positive action, demonstrating humility, taking a defenseless position, pointing out the advantage in non-conflict, and defusing the other person's violent anger.

The ANGER Train

As the conflict escalates in intensity, the relationship between the two parties deteriorates. If left unattended, each level of deterioration adds its negative emotional weight to the "Anger Train" as illustrated below.[62]

The Anger Train

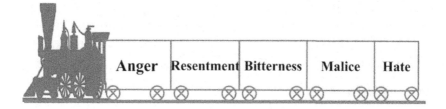

© 2012 Susan T. Gay. MMAFC; LEAD360, LLC

People often carry the heavy burden of a long train that began with *anger* toward the other person. Ecclesiastes 7:9 says, *"Be not quick in your spirit to become angry, for anger lodges in the heart of fools."*

When anger is allowed to lodge or take up residence in a person's life, it leads to *resentment*. In Ephesians 4:26-27, the Apostle Paul wrote: *"Be angry and do not sin; do not let the sun go down on your anger and give no opportunity to the devil."* Resentment is internal and personal and does not involve others. Someone has said that resentment is like taking poison and expecting the other person to die.

Resentment grows to become *bitterness*. Bitterness occurs when our resentment overflows and begins to spill over onto other people. While this may include the person we are bitter against, many times we also spread our bitterness to others around us through our bitter comments. The Bible says that bitterness "defiles many" and causes us to miss the grace of God: *"See to it that no one misses the grace of God and that no bitter root grows up to cause trouble and defile many."* (Hebrews 12:15)

146

Once our bitterness evolves to the point of *malice,* we begin to seek vengeance against the other person for their offence against us. *"Do not seek revenge or bear a grudge against one of your people, but love your neighbor as yourself. I am the LORD."* (Lev 19:18) And in Colossians 3:8 we read, *"But now you must rid yourselves of all such things as these: anger, rage, malice, slander, and filthy language from your lips."*

Ultimately, if unattended, the feeling becomes one of *hatred* for the other person, causing us to wish or even do evil toward the other person. This is defined as an act of the sinful nature in Gal. 5:20.

What's REALLY driving this train?

Anger is a secondary emotion and is not really what is driving the train. *Hurt* is the engine that drives this train.

The Hurt Train

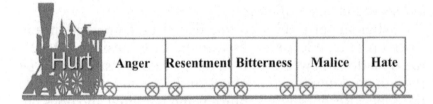

When you feel hurt by the other person, your anger can grow and degenerate to hatred because you did not deal with the original feeling of hurt. So the Anger Train is really the Hurt Train. Before you can get this train on the track to healthy conflict resolution, you must first off-load the extra weight in all those cars. The way to do that is to address the original feeling of hurt.

Two biblical perspectives on forgiveness.

If the hurt is not dealt with through forgiveness, we cannot move forward to accept the opportunities God has for us. The New Testament presents two perspectives on how to approach the need for forgiveness.

1) **Bearing with one another.** *"Therefore, as God's chosen people, holy and dearly loved, clothe yourselves with compassion, kindness, humility, gentleness and patience. Bear with each other and forgive whatever grievances you may have against one another. Forgive as the Lord forgave you. And over all these virtues put on love, which binds them all together in perfect unity. Let the peace of Christ rule in your hearts, since as members of one body you were called to peace. And be thankful."* (Colossians 3:12-15)

Bearing with one another starts with praying and thinking about the situation and the accompanying thoughts and emotions. Sometimes a problem is not important enough to expend the time and energy necessary for confrontation. For example, married couples or roommates may decide to let a lot of little things slide by bearing with one another, because they know that it is better to give grace to one another rather than making a big deal out of small issues.

You should also bear with the person if you realize that the problem is more with yourself than the other person. We all have issues and problems from our past that may cloud our present relationships. Your boss may remind you of your angry father. If you were always criticized as a child for being sloppy, an innocent comment from your spouse about picking up your dirty clothes may bother you more than it should. You may have identity issues that can cause your "buttons to be pushed." If you feel inadequate or unloved in certain situations, a word or even a look can sometimes cause those thoughts and feelings to come back. The other person did not mean to offend when she hit a sore spot in your soul that needs the healing of the Savior. In those cases, confessing your own needs or shortcomings and bearing with the other person is most appropriate.

2) Confronting. *"If your brother sins against you, go and show him his fault, just between the two of you. If he listens to you, you have won your brother over. But if he will not listen, take one or two others along, so that every matter may be established by the testimony of two or three witnesses. If he refuses to listen to them, tell it to the church; and if he refuses to listen even to the church, treat him as you would a pagan or a tax collector."* (Matthew 18:15-17)

"Therefore, if you are offering your gift at the altar and there remember that your brother has something against you, leave your gift there in front of the altar. First go and be reconciled to your brother; then come and offer your gift." (Matthew 5:23)

The first phrase from Matthew 18:15 is, *"If your brother has sinned against you..."* Again, the first step before proceeding with a biblical model of confrontation should be prayer and seeking wise counsel if needed. Did your brother or sister sin against you deliberately? It may feel like it when you consider your own hurt, but they may have just been acting the way that is natural to them from their own personality, background, and experience. Before jumping to conclusions that could make things worse, consult with a trusted third party to make sure your own motives are pure. Then confront the other person in love and if they will not respond then proceed to the next level of confrontation. Usually a conversation is needed to uncover the motive before sin can be assumed.

A good formula for that conversation is to state the facts about what happened, share how you feel or felt about what happened, and then ask a question. For example, "When you said that you did not want to socialize outside of work hours with the team, I felt really sad and hurt. May I ask why you don't want to spend time with us?" This opens a dialogue that may lead to clarification of the issues rather than a hurtful confrontation that assumes intentional wrong-doing on the other person's part. When it is clear that a sin has been committed, the Scripture is clear about how that should be handled. Start with a one-on-one conversation. Then, if no resolution is possible, bring witnesses to participate in the confrontation. If there is still no resolution, bring the issue to the church or the larger group for appropriate discipline.

The responsibility falls on the person who realizes there is a problem. If you realize that a person has sinned against you, you are to go to them. If you realize that a person is holding something against you, you are to go to them, even if it means leaving the worship service and your offering behind until the relationship is restored.

(See the chapter on "Confronting for Change.")

Levels of Conflict

Speed Leas of the Alban Institute first developed the concept of five levels of conflict intensity in the 1980s. The chart on the following two pages illustrates how the unresolved problem can grow in intensity as it degenerates to a full-blown conflict. Ultimately, it can end as an "intractable" conflict that will require intervention by a higher authority and that will lead to almost certain removal of at least one, if not both, parties. The chart can be helpful as you diagnose the intensity of the conflict and seek to take appropriate steps to resolve it.

Levels of Conflict (Chart)

	Level One: Problem to Solve	Level Two: Disagreement	Level Three: *Contest*
	Characteristics	Characteristics	Characteristics
1. ISSUE	1. Real disagreement; conflicting goals, values and needs, etc.	1. Real disagreement; mixing of personalities and issues; problem cannot be clearly defined.	1. Begin the dynamics of win/lose. Resistance to peace overtures. Focus on persons representing the enemy.
2. EMOTIONS	2. Short-lived anger, quickly controlled; parties begin to be uncomfortable in the presence of other(s) [ANGER]	2. Distrust in the beginning. Caution in association; less mixing with "the other side". [RESENTMENT]	2. Not able to operate in presence of "enemy"; however, admire worthy opponent. Not willing to share emotions/feelings constructively. [BITTERNESS]
3. ORIENTATION	3. Tends to be problem-oriented rather than person-oriented	3. Begin personalizing the problem; shrewdness and calculation begin.	3. Personal attacks. Formation of factions/sides. Threat of members leaving. Need a third-party consultant.
4. INFO	4. Open sharing of information	4. Selective hold-back of information on both sides.	4. Distortion is a major problem. Information shared only within factions.
5. LANGUAGE	5. Clear and specific	5. More vague and general; "Some people..." "They..." Hostile humor, barbed comments and put-downs.	5. Overgeneralizations: "You always..." "We never..." Attribute diabolical motives to others.
6. OBJECTIVE	6. Solving the problem. Move toward unanimous agreement. Utilize collaborative style.	6. Face-saving; come out looking good. Tend to move toward consensus. Not yet win/lose conflict.	6. Shifts from self-protection to winning. Objectives are more complex and diffuse; clustering of issues.
7. OUTCOME	7. Collaborative agreement if possible. Win/win final resolution with acceptable, mutually-agreed-upon solution.	7. Attempt a collaborative solution; or negotiate an acceptable agreement; win/win, but with a real effort.	7. Decision-making—mediation, compromising, voting. Possible that some will leave the organization.
SKILLS NEEDED	1. Trust/rapport-building skills 2. Ability to think logically 3. Good listening skills 4. Working knowledge of organization, structure, and polity 5. Problem-solving and decision-making skills 6. Consulting skills 7. Knowledge of available resources	All skills required for level one, plus... 1. Analytical skills 2. Understanding of power dynamics issues 3. Mediation skills 4. Self-awareness skills	All skills required for levels one and two, plus... 1. Designing and negotiating contracts 2. Clear recognition of one's own limits 3. Understanding interaction of personality types 4. Facilitator in group process 5. Skilled in developing a clear process of decision-making

Adapted with permission from material by Speed Leas of the Alban Institute

	Level Four: Fight/Flight	Level Five: Intractable
	Characteristics	Characteristics
1. ISSUE	1. Shifts from winning to getting rid of person(s). No longer believe others can change, nor want them to change.	1. No longer clear understanding of the issue; personalities have become the issue. Conflict is now unmanageable.
2. EMOTIONS	2. Cold self-righteousness. Will not speak to the other side. [MALICE]	2. Relentless obsession in accomplishing the objective at all costs. Vindictive. No objectivity or control of emotion. [HATRED]
3. ORIENTATION	3. Factions are solidified. Clear lines of demarcation. Last place for constructive intervention by a third-party consultant.	3. Sees person(s) as harmful to society, not just to the offended group or person.
4. INFO	4. Limited only to the cause being advocated; will not accept/listen to contrary information.	4. Information skewed to accomplish the objective at any cost.
5. LANGUAGE	5. Talk now of "principles" not "issues". Language solidifies into ideology.	5. Focuses on words that imply the destruction and/or elimination of the other.
6. OBJECTIVE	6. No longer winning; now eliminate others from the environment. Hurt the other person/group.	6. To destroy the offending party/persons; i.e., to see that the fired leader does not get a job elsewhere.
7. OUTCOME	7. High probability of split within the group with a significant number of persons leaving.	7. Highly destructive. Use of compulsion to maintain peace. May be necessary to remove one or more parties from the situation. Higher authorities may need to intervene.
SKILLS NEEDED	All skills required for previous levels plus... 1. Ability to assess need for additional skill building 2. Proven experience (track record) 3. Knowledge of broader, more specialized resources 4. Ability to find and make use of professional organizations and resources 5. Careful adherence to organizational structure and polity guidelines (legal and authority issues)	All skills required for previous levels plus... 1. Adequate personal support system and strong inner resources 2. Able to practice personal stress management 3. Careful adherence to institutional rules, boundaries, legal restrictions, authority structures, etc.

Adapted with permission from material by Speed Leas of the Alban Institute

If the conflict has already escalated beyond level three (contest), then it is very unlikely that a good resolution can be reached without someone having to leave or be dismissed.

Sometimes it is possible to take a cooling off period and allow the intensity of the conflict to decrease to the previous level before attempting to reach agreement. As you analyze the level of intensity of the conflict, give careful consideration to the Skills Needed to reach the expected Outcome for each level.

Steps toward Resolving Conflict

In their book, *Getting to Yes: Negotiating Agreement Without Giving In,* Roger Fisher and William Ury suggest four basic points of principled negotiation centering around people, interests, options, and criteria:

- People—Separate the people from the problem.
- Interests—Focus on interests not positions.
- Options—Generate a variety of possibilities before deciding what to do.
- Criteria—Insist that the result be based on some objective standard.[63]

The object is to lead people to see themselves as working together on the problem rather than against each other in competition. Rather than haggling over what either side says it will or won't do, try to identify the issues based on their merits. Look for mutual gains whenever possible. Where interests are conflicting, insist that the resolution be based on some fair standards independent of the personal desires of either side. Both sides need to listen first to understand before insisting on being heard and understood.

John Ortberg dissects Jesus' instruction in Matthew 18:15 and details seven steps for resolving conflict in his *Everybody's Normal Until You Get to Know Them*:

1) Acknowledge the conflict.
2) Own responsibility.
3) Approach, don't avoid, the other person.
4) No third parties (initially).
5) Use sensitivity.
6) Direct communication.
7) Aim at reconciliation.[64]

Reconciliation requires forgiveness. One person can decide to forgive, but unless both parties forgive, there can be no reconciliation that heals the broken relationship. Ortberg describes forgiveness as a necessary surgical procedure for restoring relationships in the community of believers. Giving up the personal right to inflict reciprocal pain on anyone who has caused hurt is the first stage of forgiveness. The second stage involves seeing the other person in a different light, and the third stage is when one begins to wish the other person well.

Confrontation, Ortberg asserts, is "the gift nobody wants." The foundational paradox is that "we want to know the truth about ourselves, and we want very much not to know the truth about ourselves. We both seek and resist awareness about the reality of who we are."[65] In spite of this paradox (or perhaps because of it), everyone needs truth-tellers who will confront in love. (Eph. 4:15) "We need others to help us live up to our best intentions and deepest values" to avoid living in *pseudocommunity* where there is a strict avoidance of conflict.[66]

Building community requires both bonding and bridging. "Bonding happens when people who perceive themselves to be similar develop deeper connections; but bridging activities involve people who have been separated."[67] Jesus, Ortberg notes, was the greatest bridge-builder. His commands to his followers to love one another and to forgive one another provide the secret to building community such as the world has never seen. Again, love is the key to restoring and maintaining unity and harmony in any body of believers. If they know you care, then you can confront effectively in love. (We discuss more about confronting in love in the chapter on "Confronting for Change")

But my workplace is not a church!

The beauty of these principles is in the fact that they transcend cultural context and can be applied by Christians in any conflict situation—in the church, at home, and in the secular workplace. The same basic approach to conflict management or conflict resolution can be applied in any setting. Teams led by Christian leaders in the church or in the workplace should be a model of unity within the community of the team. When the people you lead know that you genuinely care for them, it is amazing how much more likely it is that they will respond positively when confronted. As we actively make peace, we are building *unity* in *community* and that will result in more fruit for the Kingdom.

Confronting for Change
Guidelines for dealing with difficult personnel issues

"The Lord's bond-servant must not be quarrelsome, but be kind to all, able to teach, patient when wronged..."
(2 Timothy 2:24 (NASB))

"...Warn those who are idle, encourage the timid, help the weak, be patient with everyone. Make sure that nobody pays back wrong for wrong, but always try to be kind to each other and to everyone else."
(1 Thessalonians 5:12-15)

"Failure to deal with the problems people and organizations face can be the most unloving action of all."
(Leith Anderson)

155

156

> ## Servant-stewards know how to confront appropriately.
>
> - Servant-stewards know when to engage and when not to engage. (1 Tim. 4:2-3; 1 Tim. 5:20)
> - Servant-stewards choose their battles, and then fight their battles well. (1 Tim. 6:11-20)
> - Servant-stewards are willing to confront appropriately and in a timely manner when necessary, for both the good of the individual as well as the good of the body. (2 Tim. 2:22-26; 3:1-9)
> - Servant-stewards seek the correction of behaviors and not the destruction of individuals. (1 Tim. 5:20)
> - Servant-stewards show patience and love when it is necessary to correct others. (2 Tim. 3:10-11)
> - Servant-stewards recognize the fact that anyone can fall unless they stay on the right path all the time. (1 Tim. 1:20)
> - Servant-stewards recognize that not everyone can be rescued. (2 Tim. 2:17, 18; Titus 3:10-11)
> - Servant-stewards are willing to make the hard decisions when necessary and at the appropriate time. (Titus 3:10-11; 2 Tim. 2:24-26)

Count the Cost

After a year on the job, Jarod[68] and his boss, Alex, did not see eye to eye on everything. In fact, they probably saw most things differently. Even so, Jarod made a conscious effort not to speak negatively in public or with other workers when referring to his work situation. He was surprised that he had never had a performance evaluation, especially since he knew the company policy clearly stipulated that reviews should take place at six and twelve months after a new employee began work. Although he wasn't completely happy in his new job, as far as Jarod could tell, he was adequately fulfilling his responsibilities.

That's why it caught him completely by surprise on Friday morning when Alex stepped into his office and announced, "You know, this really is not working out well, so today is your last day here. Clean out your desk and turn in all your pending files by this afternoon."[69]

Unfortunately, Jarod's story is not very unusual among many businesses. Some organizations act as if they believe leadership is a natural, innate ability that is automatically imparted to anyone named to any management position.

One of the first items to be cut during difficult financial times is training for leaders. Small businesses and non-profit organizations are often notorious for providing less than adequate training and skills upgrade for leaders. Cutting leadership training from the budget might appear to provide short-term budget savings, but the long-term results will be very costly. Consider the cost of poor leadership as it results in reduced productivity, decline in morale, erasure of loyalty, and increased personnel costs.[70]

1. Reduced productivity.

How much productivity is lost by people talking about the problems caused by a weak or a dominating leader? People will always spend time talking around the actual or figurative "water cooler." Poor leadership is likely to ensure that the conversation is negative and counterproductive. Much time and energy can be lost agonizing over the poor decisions and poor interpersonal skills of leaders.

2. Decline in Morale

Who wants to work in a place where you don't know what's expected and you never know when the axe might fall? Poor morale grows like mold in the darkness and is not easily turned around.

3. Erasure of loyalty

Loyalty has become a thing of the past. Employees do not demonstrate loyalty to the company because they do not feel loyalty *from* the company to its employees. Managers seem to forget that the organization cannot reach its objectives without the productive participation of its personnel. Loyalty is built on trust and trust is built on trustworthiness. Employees who do not trust their leader/supervisors will tend to adhere strictly to the rules, regulations, and policies out of fear. One union worker once told me that the way to shut a company down is for the workers to apply the letter of the law and follow every policy to the letter.

4. Increased personnel costs

Often leaders draw the bottom line too soon when "counting the cost." Consider the high cost of not confronting or dealing with the problem. Consider the cost of severance packages, searching for and hiring new personnel to fill vacancies, and the cost of collateral losses when other people quit or become less productive because they can't seem to get along with the individual who is causing problems.

Remember the Reason

"No discipline seems pleasant at the time, but painful. Later on, however, it produces a harvest of righteousness and peace for those who have been trained by it." (Hebrews 12:11)

One of the greatest obstacles to effective care-fronting is the inability to say "no" to the demands of others. Because we are finite beings trapped in time and space, we simply cannot say "yes" to everything. Whenever you say "yes" to anything, you are automatically saying "no" to everything else that might have taken up your time and energy. The solution for those who have trouble saying "no" is to say "yes" to your values. By saying "yes" first to a greater value, it can become easier to say no when someone makes a demand that threatens or imposes on that value.

Learning to confront effectively means taking the long view, keeping your values at the forefront as these shape your decisions. It then becomes easier to do what is right because it is right. Effective confrontation should be offered caringly, gently, constructively, acceptingly, and clearly. If they know you care, then you can confront effectively in love.

Confrontational meetings are always best done through personal and direct forms of communication and followed up in writing. At every point along the way, remember that as a leader, you already have authority and a certain power that can easily be misused. You do not have to be mean as you exercise leadership to help someone become a more effective worker within the bounds of the organization's vision, mission, objectives, and policies. You do not have to be "bossy" or use command language to get the person to change a specific unacceptable behavior. **It is important that the person confronted senses that you, as their leader, want them to succeed, and that you believe they can. The goal is to communicate clearly that this person is of value and can be a productive and effective team member by changing the specific behavior or attitude you are addressing.** If the other person can see your face and hear your voice of compassion as you communicate the difficult words, there is a better chance of achieving the goal of change.

> **Servant-stewards are blatantly biblical in the way they define and apply any authority.**
> - Servant-stewards know how to correctly use Scripture to equip themselves and others for effective ministry. (2 Tim. 3:14-4:8)
> - Servant-stewards are careful about how and when to use Scripture when applying corrective action while maintaining a strong biblical foundation for all they do. (2 Tim. 2:22-26; 3:1-9; 3:14-4:8)

So, What Can You Do?

Years ago, Tom Peters suggested in *Thriving on Chaos* that policies should express positive expectations.[71] Try to make policies that enable, empower, and motivate people to respond with service. Limit negative policies to the absolute minimum. Avoid writing policies based on one or two negative experiences. Most organizations or companies have written policies and procedures for how to carry out administrative actions with personnel who are not performing to management's expectations. The mere publication of a policy and procedure, however, does not guarantee that managers know how to effectively administer personnel issues to the best benefit of the organization. Training is needed to help leaders learn how to administer policies in such a way that the productivity of their personnel actually improves.

Whether or not Jarod was performing his duties satisfactorily to Alex's expectations, there are a few simple steps that Alex could have followed that could have resulted in a much happier ending to Jarod's story for all concerned. The steps are simple, but they do require some effort.

One of the most painful requirements of leadership is the necessity to take administrative action to correct an individual's unacceptable behavior or failure to meet the expectations of their job assignment. Much of the pain can be averted, however, if the leader will follow some very simple principles of early intervention at the first signs of trouble.

Confront the Problem Early

Start with a clear job description. In many cases, the problem develops because the leader was not clear in expressing specific expectations that individuals should meet in their job assignments. Clear expectations from the beginning can solve many personnel problems before they begin. As individuals advance in their assignment, continue to dialogue about expectations and make sure you are both in agreement on these.

Harold Schoenberg said, "Anybody who gets away with something will come back to get away with a little bit more." A researcher friend was contracted by a large organization to review over twenty years of documents related to their most serious personnel issues to see if there were any common factors and then to make recommendations for improvements. She concluded that the most important common issue was this: **every one of them had multiple interventions due to serious problems that should have been resolved much sooner**. Don't fall into the trap of waiting until you reach the end of your rope to finally deal with the problem or, worse, until it turns into a full-blown personnel crisis.

Leaders often find it difficult to confront appropriately when an individual's behavior is affecting their performance or relationships on the team. As the unresolved problem continues to grow, the team finds itself consuming more and more time and emotional energy dealing with this individual's problem, putting a drag on everyone's performance. Although the leader might view confrontation as undesirable, in fact, "Failure to deal with the problems people and organizations face can be the most unloving action of all."[72] Good stewardship demands that leaders confront issues as early as possible with the hope of helping the person correct an unacceptable behavior or attitude before it becomes a terminable offense.

Confront with Purpose

How you, as the leader, confront the problem is crucial. Someone has said, "There are no problem people, only people with problems." Tom Elliff quoted his grandmother who said, "Be nice to everyone because everyone has problems." You must first see the individual as a person who needs help. At the same time, you must be careful to consider your own motives when confronting individuals. Never assume that the person is aware of the problem and already knows how to correct it. It is your responsibility as a leader to confront the individual first with an attitude of helping to correct a problem for the good of the individual, their coworkers, and the work of the organization.

The New Testament provides clear advice to help leaders lessen the agony that comes when difficult decisions must be made regarding personnel issues:

> *"If your brother sins against you, go and show him his fault, just between the two of you. If he listens to you, you have won your brother over. But if he will not listen, take one or two others along, so that 'every matter may be established by the testimony of two or three witnesses.' If he refuses to listen to them, tell it to the church; and if he refuses to listen even to the church, treat him as you would a pagan or a tax collector. I tell you the truth, whatever you bind on earth will be bound in heaven, and whatever you loose on earth will be loosed in heaven. Again, I tell you that if two of you on earth agree about anything you ask for, it will be done for you by my Father in heaven. For where two or three come together in my name, there am I with them."* (Mt. 18:15-20)

"Now we ask you, brothers, to respect those who work hard among you, who are over you in the Lord and who admonish you. Hold them in the highest regard in love because of their work. Live in peace with each other. And we urge you, brothers, warn those who are idle, encourage the timid, help the weak, be patient with everyone. Make sure that nobody pays back wrong for wrong, but always try to be kind to each other and to everyone else." (1 Thess. 5:12-15)

"Keep reminding them of these things. Warn them before God against quarreling about words; it is of no value, and only ruins those who listen. Do your best to present yourself to God as one approved, a workman who does not need to be ashamed and who correctly handles the word of truth. Avoid godless chatter, because those who indulge in it will become more and more ungodly. Their teaching will spread like gangrene." (2 Tim. 2:14-17a)

"But avoid foolish controversies and genealogies and arguments and quarrels about the law, because these are unprofitable and useless. Warn a divisive person once, and then warn him a second time. After that, have nothing to do with him. You may be sure that such a man is warped and sinful; he is self-condemned." (Titus 3:9-11)

"If anyone does not obey our instruction in this letter, take special note of him. Do not associate with him, in order that he may feel ashamed. Yet do not regard him as an enemy, but warn him as a brother." (2 Thess. 3:14-15)

The New Testament pattern seems to be consistent. From the moment the personnel problem first becomes evident, the goal is to restore the relationship and maintain unity in the Body. When problems of performance or unacceptable behavior arise, these must be addressed. Leaders have a stewardship responsibility to confront both unacceptable behavior and failure to meet expectations and to deal with these in a way that adheres to company policies and guidelines, complies with any legal requirements or restrictions, and at the same time conforms to biblical principles. Sometimes that might seem like juggling three balls at once, but it can be done.

On his first day as a shop manager, Marcus[73] asked if the former manager had any advice for him. "Yeah. You will have to do something about Bob," he warned. "Bob has been a problem for a long time and his sour attitude affects everybody in the shop. I apologize for leaving this one for you, but it's past time to take action."

"So what do you suggest?" asked Marcus.

"Right off the bat, first thing, why don't you go up to him and say, 'You know, Bob, you really aren't happy here, are you?' He is sure to say, no he is not. So then you can say, 'Well wouldn't you be happier someplace else?' and when he says, yes, you can offer to help him out the door."

Marcus took the advice, went straight to Bob and said, "Bob, you really aren't happy here, are you?" to which Bob replied, "Nope."

"So, you would probably be happier working someplace else, wouldn't you."

"I would. That's right. Yeah! And you know what? I'm gonna do something about that. I QUIT!"

Marcus helped him pack his tools right then and walked with him out the door to the audible sighs of relief from the rest of the workers in the shop.

Not every confrontation goes that easily. But when you confront with a gentle, yet firm and confident spirit it will always go better than with harshness where it is difficult to see the Spirit of Christ shining through. As the supervisor, you already have the position of power, so you don't have to be mean about it.

Caution! Personalities at work.

Before approaching any confrontational conversation, look over your Birkman reports (both your own and the other person's). Everyone in the room will be bringing their own personality with their own unique perspective to the entire situation, so put all your emotional intelligence to work. Ideally, you should have the other person's "Personal User Manual" with their own summary statements. Consider how the other person's behaviors might not correspond to your Needs/expectations that could result in your feeling stressed. Knowing this can help you to compensate and avoid falling into your less effective, Stress behavior.

Also, give some thought to how your own behaviors might cause the other person stress since they might not be how the other person needs or expects others to behave toward them. Just because they are acting a certain way does not mean they want or expect others to behave the same way toward them. Try to adjust your demeanor to match their Need. This can help them to stay in their own most effective, Usual style. If you concentrate on creating an environment that provides what they need to help them use their more positive and effective style of behavior, you will increase the probability of a positive outcome from the meeting.

Document, Document, Document

Experienced leaders know the first rule of any administrative action is "Document, Document, Document." Often when a difficult administrative action must be taken, there is little or no documentation in the file to justify or back up the decision that should be made. Then, when things seem to have gone beyond the point of tolerance, the leader finds themself either having to go back and recreate a history of the problem or having to slow down the process and begin documenting starting at a point where more serious action should be taking place already.

On the one hand, by documenting the problem from the beginning, both the leader and the individual will have a clear view of just how long the unacceptable behavior or attitude has been a problem and just how much this problem is affecting the work of the individual and of others around them. When it is time to take administrative action, the leader can use the accurate documentation to remind the individual exactly when and what observations were made and what steps have been taken up to this point to try and help them correct the unacceptable behavior and meet the expectations of the job.

There is the need for documentation from a legal standpoint. In a worst-case scenario, if someone is about to be terminated for failure to perform, there must be a "paper trail" to show what has warranted such drastic administrative action and what steps have been taken to help the individual correct their unacceptable behavior or attitude.

A major question that upper level leadership will always ask is, "What steps have been taken prior to this action?" In the case of termination, it is extremely important to show how the problem is affecting the work, how it has been confronted, and what the leader has done previously to attempt to correct the unacceptable behavior.

Keep accurate records, not only to cover yourself in case of appeals or litigation, but also as a record to help everyone remember the same things. It will help your upline leadership follow a timeline of events. Additionally, when there is any leadership change, the new leaders can also be brought up to speed more easily through your accurate documentation. This can help to prevent passing unresolved problems from team to team through transfers.

In the Appendix we have included a suggested outline, "Confronting for Change—Step by Step".

When the Confrontation is Not Well Taken

Be clear, be firm, and be nice... all at the same time.

Some people will not accept correction with grace. Some of these will insist that they have been misunderstood or mistreated and will not see the need to correct their behavior or attitude. While it is normal to feel embarrassed when an unacceptable behavior or attitude has been pointed out, personnel who make threats, argue incessantly, or repeatedly try to call in "bigger guns" to defend their position are giving evidence of deeper issues that need to be addressed. In some cases, there may be underlying emotional wellness issues that should be considered and dealt with by a trained counselor.

These types of reactions require a firm and loving response. When following up with such individuals, always stay on topic and reiterate the original decision in a calm and loving manner, no matter what the reaction may be. The person will likely appeal the decision to other levels of leadership. You should be familiar with your organization's policies regarding appeals so that, if asked, you can inform the applicant of the appropriate persons to contact. The appropriate leaders should be well-informed and understand the nature of the decision in case of appeal.

Be confident and maintain confidentiality

As a leader and representative of the organization, you should always maintain a high level of confidentiality, even if the individual does not tell the truth about why they were confronted. This is especially true in cases that lead to termination. Do not succumb to the temptation to "set the record straight" when an individual appears to have distorted the truth about why they are leaving. When well-meaning friends, co-workers ,or even other leaders attempt to intervene on the individual's behalf, keep in mind that maintaining confidentiality is not simply a legal responsibility. If confidences are broken or violated, word will soon spread and trust will be broken that will undermine your ability to lead effectively until the trust can be rebuilt.

What DOESN'T work

There are several *ineffective* ways to approach confrontation. The following list is adapted from *Who's Pushing Your Buttons, Handling the Difficult People*, by Dr. John Townsend.[74]

1. Carrot or Stick.

The carrot or stick approach implies a general unwillingness to comply with the demands made by others. Through the offer of rewards for good behavior or punishment for bad behavior, the carrot or stick approach amounts to coercion. At best it will result in compliance. There is always a risk, however, that when the anticipation of the reward or the fear of the punishment is no longer present, the individual will stop complying or revert back to the unacceptable behavior.

2. Reasoning with the Unreasonable

Some people simply will not listen. When you disagree, that becomes a signal for them to tune you out. No amount of reasoning will convince them to change their mind.

3. Separating Truth from Grace

Grace is defined as unmerited favor. Truth is what *is*, what is *real*. Both are necessary and need each other to be effective. Truth without love and grace that ignores reality are both ineffective. Truth without love can be seen as harsh and selfish. If we administer only grace, then we can fall into patterns of enabling bad behavior.

4. Enabling

Like families of addicts, the enabler makes excuses for the other person's bad behavior or covers for them. This only allows the problem to continue and become worse.

5. Nagging

While people need to be reminded, nagging ultimately makes things worse. Just don't do it!

6. Threatening with no Follow-up

This also makes things worse. When threats are made with no follow-up action, the bad behavior is reinforced. Townsend counsels, "[I]f you bark, be prepared to bite. If you aren't, get yourself a muzzle!"[75]

7. Denial (ignoring the problem)

This is the "head in the sand" approach. Like the three monkeys, "See no Evil, Hear no Evil, and Speak no Evil," ignoring, avoiding, or denying that the problem exists will not make it any better. If you have doubts about whether to confront or how and when, seek the advice of a safe, trusted, and truthful friend to see if they feel the problem should be addressed.

8. One Time Should Do It

Most people need to be reminded. Just because you told them does not necessarily mean they will remember. While you want to be careful not to nag, you do want to communicate clearly and that usually requires repetition.

9. Spiritualizing

It is good for you and the person being confronted to be spiritual people. *Spiritualizing,* however, is really rooted in pride. Instead of simply *living* the Word, you begin to sound "preachy." Praying and hoping are good and right, but some people become passive and withdraw from taking any action when action is required. Spiritualizing can also lead to an attitude of superiority, where the person feels they are closer to God than others and they are unable to relate to others in earthly ways. Spiritualizing may also be a way to divert attention and avoid dealing with practical or interpersonal issues.

10. Taking too much Responsibility

It is easy to begin to think that the fault for the problem is really all on you: "If only I had done something differently." The other person might also try to place all the blame on you, insisting that your unreasonable demands made it impossible for them to comply. Take reasonable responsibility for the problem, but don't feel totally, personally, irrevocably responsible for everything. That's God's job.

11. Waiting for Permission

While this sounds polite and respectful, it can be a long wait. In effect, this is placing all the responsibility on the other person when the other person might never feel the need to address the problem. If you are waiting for somebody to take the first step toward a solution, remember, you are somebody.

12. Reacting and Blasting

We all have "hot buttons." When the other person presses one, especially if we are already under stress, we are likely to react out of stress in a negative or immature way. You can't control the initial reaction you feel. You can, however, control how you will respond. That initial reaction is a stress behavior. Respond from your more effective style.

Receiving Confrontation

What if you are in the uncomfortable position of being the one who is confronted? Winston Churchill is often quoted as having said, "I am always ready to learn although I do not always like being taught." No one enjoys being corrected. It is up to you, however, to decide what your attitude will be in response to the confrontation. Give the other person the benefit of doubt and try to assume that they want the best for you. This is an opportunity to grow. Ask the other person to help you with any blind spots that might have led to the current situation and to help you make the necessary correction to grow and do better from this point forward.

<u>Leadership Hints</u>

The following are general suggestions to take into account when confronting for change. For detailed steps to follow in a process of confrontation, see the "Take Action" section below.

1. Always pray before confronting.

Ask God to give wisdom, discernment, and guidance to help you communicate clearly both what needs to change and why the change is necessary. Pray for a calm spirit.

2. Clarify expectations.

If a worker is not meeting your expectations, confront early to make this known. All too often leaders wait until the problem becomes so unbearable that they suddenly turn into the Incredible Hulk and go ballistic without warning. They hold their complaints until they scream out like Popeye in the cartoons, "That's all I can stands, I can't stands no more!" And the next thing you know he is beating up on Brutus like a tornado. You might think you are demonstrating patience by holding your comments, but you are really doing the person a disservice by not letting them know clearly what the consequences will be if agreed upon expectations are not met. Make your expectations clear from the beginning. Let them know what a good job should look like.

3. Offer assistance for improvement.

If the individual is not performing to the level of your expectations, assume the first responsibility and make sure they receive adequate instruction and training. Consider a coaching approach to supervision. Ask questions and LISTEN CAREFULLY to be sure you understand what the problem is. Make sure the individual has an accountability partner for progress.

4. When giving a warning, clearly outline the consequences of failure to meet expectations. Then offer more assistance.

Be careful to avoid using "warning language" too early. You should only use warning language when you are having to deal with the same issues a second or third time.

Many leaders want to skip this step and just go straight to the final corrective administrative action—also known as "You're fired!" Unless the failure is clearly a terminal offense, give a clear warning that this behavior or attitude is unacceptable and must be changed or there will be further corrective action that could lead to termination. Ask if there is anything keeping the individual from being able to meet the expectation. Offer to provide additional help such as a mentor or coach. KEEP LISTENING.

5. Get help for yourself, too.

Everyone needs a mentor, coach, advisor, counselor, accountability partner, or friend who can offer a listening ear, ask questions, give an opinion or offer suggestions. Ask if you are being reasonable or if there might be an alternative that could possibly get better results. Consult up line with your own leader to be sure you are standing on solid ground and will have the support of your leader if corrective action is required. Your supervisor should always be given a "heads up" that a problem could be brewing.

6. Set a specific date for review.

Be sure the individual knows not only what is expected, but also when it is expected and when they will give you an accounting of progress.

7. Reward baby steps.

The reward can be very simple and very small. As in horse training, often the most effective reward is a very small positive stimulus to a very small movement in the right direction. The reward can be as simple as releasing the tension on the reins when the horse first makes even a slight nudge of the head in the right direction. In the beginning, reward or praise even the intent to correct the unacceptable behavior. Be careful, however, not to over-praise which can be seen as insincerity.

8. Redirect a thought.

Cowboys know that a cornered steer will cut its eyes in the direction of a perceived escape. An experienced rider will move to block that thought and make the escape route seem uninviting by waving a hand with a hat or a lasso or pulling the horse in the path of visibility to make the space seem smaller and less secure. As soon as you see an unacceptable behavior, find a way to redirect the person's thinking or behavior to something positive and acceptable.

9. Follow up.

Even if the unacceptable behavior or performance is corrected, follow up to let them know you remember and truly expect a change to take place. Ask about progress along the way. Be sure they know you want them to succeed. (You *do* want them to succeed, don't you?) After a face-to-face, phone call, or video conference meeting, follow up with an email confirming in writing what you talked about. Remind them of what you agreed upon and your specific expectations.

To be sure you are communicating clearly and documenting the conversation accurately, a good practice can be to write your email to the individual *before* the conversation, *but do not send it yet!* Use this as a guide or basic script for your conversation. Then, after the conversation, make any changes, additions or corrections based on the actual conversation. Send the email *after* the conversation. When you say in the email. "As we discussed..." or "to confirm our conversation..." you can be more confident that this really was what you said. To keep from accidentally sending the email before you are ready, don't add any addresses until *after* the meeting.

Other than specific points that need to be relayed verbatim, be careful not to sound as if you are reading from a script—even though you do want to stay close to the script you have prepared. Try your best to communicate your sincere desire to help the individual see your desire to help them succeed and that for this to happen, specific changes must take place.

10. Follow through.

Never give a warning unless you are fully prepared to follow through with action. Threats do not produce better results or more productive behavior. Be a person of integrity whose actions align with your words. Don't threaten to do anything. Instead, let it be known what the consequences will be and then act exactly as you say you will.

11. Not all attrition is bad.

As much as we might dislike letting people go, sometimes it is for the best. Even your best efforts to help some people align their behaviors, attitudes and, actions with the vision, mission, values, and strategy of the team and the organization will not succeed. If the individual insists on going their own way and it is being disruptive to the work, then the best and most loving action for all is to part company.

Followership Hints

What if my supervisor is not following these steps? How do I deal with an inconsiderate or incompetent supervisor?

1. Pray for your leaders.

Imagine how much difference it could make if we actually prayed for our leaders more than we complain about them.

2. Go the extra mile.

Show that you really are trying to do the best job possible with what you have been given.

3. Make suggestions instead of demands.

Let your supervisor know you really do want to help make things better, not just for yourself, but also for the benefit of the work or ministry.

4. Be respectful.

Be careful not to develop an attitude of disdain or arrogance. Even if you think your supervisor is not doing a good job, they are still your supervisor and deserve respect.

5. Model the behavior you want your supervisor to demonstrate toward you.

Be courteous. If you want more communication, communicate more. If you want more openness, be more open.

6. Recognize that not all personalities are created the same.

Some people are more people oriented, some are more task oriented. Some prefer more direct communication while others prefer more indirect ways of communicating. Try to adapt to your supervisor's way of doing things while also asking them to recognize your personality differences.

7. Ask for training. Ask for help.

Recognize your need for development. You might need to find your own mentor, coach, or accountability partner. Don't just use them to vent your frustrations. Ask them to help you set goals for real improvement and growth.

8. Ultimately, you are responsible for seeing that your needs are met.

Don't expect someone else to be responsible for your personal development and growth. Take responsibility for your own career.

9. If the supervisor does not follow up in writing, follow up in writing yourself.

Allow time for the supervisor to follow up, but if the follow-up correspondence does not come in a timely manner, write a courteous email thanking them for the meeting and explain that this is what you understood from that conversation.[76]

Responding for Health
Helping hurting people in crisis

"In time of crisis people want to know that you care,
more than they care what you know."
(Will Rogers)'

"The LORD is my shepherd; I shall not want...
Even though I walk through the valley
of the shadow of death,
I will fear no evil, for you are with me;
your rod and your staff, they comfort me."
(Psalm 23:1-4)

"And let our people learn to devote themselves to good
works, so as to help cases of urgent need, and not be
unfruitful."
(Titus 3:14)

Although this will be the shortest chapter in this handbook, it is by no means the least important. Responding for Health means responding in love to the crises personnel face. Consult with your leadership and become familiar with your organization's policies defining contingency plans and who is responsible for different kinds of decisions that must be made. In any crisis, you need to be able to respond quickly and decisively with the confidence that you have the organization backing you up. To do that, you need to know your own limits as defined by the following:

1. The organizational structure, policies, and guidelines
2. Your job description
3. Your supervisor's expectations
4. Your personal boundaries, expectations and limitations

Dealing with Crises

Frontline leaders are first responders when crisis hits, providing initial help for personnel and their families who experience any crisis or trauma. You will need to work with your HR department and leadership to plan contingencies for any crisis including the following:

Death of a loved one

Major illness

Personal injury (accidental, personal violence, war)

Forced Relocation

Sexual harassment or assault

Abuse

Abductions (personally being held hostage or when family members or close friends are taken)

Victims of violent acts (or witnesses to violent acts)

Natural disasters (Any workers volunteering to help in a disaster zone should not be allowed to stay more than two weeks at a time without taking a significant break away from the affected area.)

War (PTSD and secondary PTSD can result from living through the effects of war. The trauma can be just as great whether they experienced it themselves or worked over any period of time with war victims.)

Avoid burnout

I heard a trainer say to a group of new leaders, "Burn yourself out for Jesus." I immediately countermanded that order and told the group, "If you burn yourself out, you will be no good to me, to the people you are supposed to be leading, to the people we serve, or to Jesus. I don't want candles that have burned out; I want lamps that will go on shining in the darkness." Burned out leaders cause more collateral damage than their good work can compensate. They become stressed out and then begin to infect others with stress.

Being a good steward includes the stewardship of the body you occupy. So take care of yourself. Get adequate rest, eat well, exercise regularly, maintain a good spiritual discipline that includes Bible study, prayer, and solitude. Take regular days off and extended vacations. Set a good example and be a good steward of the relationships with the people in your spheres of influence.

Living in the reality of a litigious society

A bumper sticker made a true commentary on American society today: "Hit me. I already have the papers ready to file." Another followed the same thought: "There are three ways to get rich: Inherit it, work for it, or SUE for it!" (They forgot to mention the lottery—but I digress...) We are inundated with ads for lawyers on broadcast television and outdoor advertisements, raising the same expectations as ads for casinos. The popular culture has bred and spread the idea that "someone else is always to blame and therefore I deserve to have it all." By doing what is right because it is right and following solidly biblical principles as you model a servant-steward attitude in your leadership role, you will minimize the potential risk of lawsuits.

Know When to Refer and to Whom

At some point, you will find yourself in over your head and will need to refer a supervisee for some professional intervention. It might be to a counselor, a coach, or some other personnel resource provided by the organization. Consult with your HR department for guidance on how to follow your company's guidelines for making referrals. If you do not have a referral policy already in place, use the following draft to craft your own guideline in consultation with a professional HR consultant and legal counsel.

Administrative Referrals for Counseling

Definition:

Administrative Referral refers to anyone in direct-line supervision instructing an individual to contact a counselor because of what appears to be an emotional or behavioral

180

problem that is interfering significantly with work performance and might be helped with counseling. In the case of Administrative Referral, the individual is not independently seeking the help of the counselor (at least, not to the knowledge of the leader concerned), and the supervisor sees the need for a specific and significant change or improvement in work performance that might be achieved with the help of counseling.

If a team member appears to be having problems that bother them but that do not interfere with their work performance and pose no threat to the future of the work, then the leader might choose to remind such a person that counseling might be helpful, but Administrative Referral would not be in order in such cases.

Reasons for Referral

Some possible reasons for referral include but are not limited to the following:
- Pervasive attitudes or patterns of behavior that frequently and significantly interfere with the individual's performance on the team or create disturbance and distraction in team, ministry, or other arenas of life and work. This might include anger, hostility, negativity, argumentativeness, aggressive behavior, lack of assertiveness that frequently and significantly interfere with individual or team performance.
- Specific emotional or psychological problems that significantly interfere with work performance, such as specific phobias, anxiety, depression or addiction.
- Culture shock, language learning problems, and adjustment problems that do not respond to other support and guidance.
- Traumatic incidents should always generate an immediate referral.

How to Refer

A letter should be written to the counselor informing them of the referral. Appropriate people should be copied (check with your leadership and HR department). This letter should contain (1) a clear statement of the expectation that the individual will contact the counselor with any dates or deadlines that were set for making contact, (2) a description of the problem behavior as you observe it, (3) a description of the desired change, and (4) expectations for reporting. Usually a general statement by the counselor is sufficient. The counselor will need a release form from the employee to give information to the supervisor. Other administrative matters of concern, but not directly related to the issue, should be addressed to other appropriate persons by separate communication.

And Finally...

As Paul was signing off his last letter to Timothy, he recounted how he had faced persecution for standing up for his beliefs and speaking out boldly:

> *At my first defense no one came to stand by me, but all deserted me. May it not be charged against them! But the Lord stood by me and strengthened me, so that through me the message might be fully proclaimed and all the Gentiles might hear it. So I was rescued from the lion's mouth. The Lord will rescue me from every evil deed and bring me safely into his heavenly kingdom. To him be the glory forever and ever. Amen.* (2 Tim. 4:16-18)

You might feel you are swimming upstream against society as you follow these principles and characteristics of servant-stewardship. But if you are faithful to the One to Whom you belong, the rewards will be worth the effort. You can be bold without being brash. You can be confident without being cocky. You can provide meaningful leadership in your workplace without being mean. You can be a fruitful servant by being a faithful steward.

May God bless you as you seek to be a faithful *servant-steward* of all He has been, is, and will be placing under your administration. As Paul would say in closing his letters to Timothy and Titus, "Grace be with you."

Larry and Susan Gay
www.MyLEAD360.com
LEAD360@gmail.com

PART TWO

The Pastoral Epistles – Group Exegesis

Goal of the study:

Discover the character and characteristics of supervisors as described in Scripture, specifically from Paul's letters to Timothy and Titus. Throughout the three letters, Paul establishes principles for spiritual leadership and Christian behavior in general as being rooted in the gospel. These principles should be applicable to any Christian in any leadership position—especially those who are supervising others—regardless of the setting or circumstances.[77]

1 Timothy

1 Timothy 1:1-11

1 Tim. 1:1-2

1. **Servant-stewards see their role as more than a job—it is a calling.**

   Paul reminds Timothy that he (Paul) has been given a responsibility under orders from God. He refers to himself as an *apostle* (a sent one, or "missionary"), writing to Timothy as his spiritual child. The specific word "my" does not appear in the Greek texts anywhere to Timothy or Titus, so *true child in the faith* or "true son" could also imply "a true child of God." His opening to the letter to Titus is very similar. He also refers to Titus as his true child in the faith. (Titus 1:4)

188

2. **Servant-stewards are blatantly biblical in the way they define and apply any authority.**

   They know how to use God's Word appropriately in their daily lives and apply it appropriately in their leadership roles. They do not see authority as something that is within them as a person, but it is derived from the authority of Scripture. They never have to say, "Because I say so" or "Because I'm the boss!"
   (See numbers 65, 66)

3. **Servant-stewards demonstrate the power of the presence of the Spirit in their demeanor, not "lording it over others."**
   (See numbers 9, 63, 22)

   1 Tim. 1:3
4. **Servant-stewards are player-coaches.**
   (See number 53)

   The fact that Paul left Timothy in Ephesus as he (Paul) was on the way to Macedonia indicates that he was still active in the ministry (likely between imprisonments).

   1 Tim. 1:3-4
5. **Servant-stewards have an observably close walk with the Lord.**
   (See numbers 13, 50)

   Paul trusted Timothy to know right from wrong. They had walked together and worked side-by-side for an extended time, so Paul had seen Timothy in action and knew he had a close relationship with the Lord.

1 Tim. 1:3-4

6. **Servant-stewards demonstrate their trustworthiness to make good decisions based on knowing right from wrong.**
(see numbers 17, 56, 72)

7. **Servant-stewards understand their stewardship responsibility that comes from God by faith.**

    Paul saw his calling as a stewardship responsibility to God. He saw himself as a steward of God's Word, of the gospel that he had been called to preach to the Gentile world, and of the people whom he had been entrusted to lead. (see also 1 Tim. 4:14) Titus 1:7)

1 Tim. 1:5-7

8. **Servant-stewards know how to confront appropriately.**
(See numbers 6, 7, 24, 38, 58, 63)

    Paul defined three foundational pillars of spiritual leadership that flow out of love:
    1) *A pure heart*
    2) *A good conscience* (= good character)
    3) *A sincere faith*
    Discernment flows from these. Their understanding of what is important is birthed from their relationship with God and comes from God's Spirit.
    They can distinguish between good, healthy disagreements, and important issues on which there must be unity or conformity. They can take a stand on clear doctrinal issues based on Scripture while not allowing themselves to become embroiled in matters of personal preference or speculation.

9. **Servant-stewards demonstrate a genuine love for the people they lead.**
(See numbers 25, 34)

Agape - love that shows patience, kindness. It is important that people know their leaders love them. "You don't have to be mean if you already have the authority." (Jn. 15:13)

1 Tim. 1:8-10
10. **Servant-stewards focus on positive goals.**

They are characterized by what they are for, not what they are against. Leading from the positive, there is no need to be legalistic. (See numbers 15, 54; see also 2 Tim. 4:16-17.)

11. **The best supervisors build a culture of people who are not obsessed by the law or policies, but who see the practicality of *principles* which underlie the law.**
(see number 54) (see Titus 2:1-14; 3:9)

You cannot list enough things to get people to do what is right. We're not trying to catch them doing wrong, we're trying to train them to do right. (*the law is not... for the just, but for the...disobedient...*)

1 Tim. 1:12-17

12. Supervisors should be chosen based on clear evidence of God's call in their lives.

(See numbers 5, 16, 29)

Leadership is often viewed as a reward for good work, for service or for success; but God rewards faithfulness. We need a career path that rewards people who stay on the frontline. Not everyone should be in an administrative or leadership role. Leadership should be based on gifting and the individual's identity in Christ.

1 Tim. 1:16-17

13. Servant-stewards recognize their need for the grace of God (mercy) as the basis for their success.

(See number 188, 50)

Patience. Paul declared that Jesus was using him to display his (Jesus') patience for his own sake and for his glory. Paul put himself forward as an example of how God works in imperfect individuals to accomplish what God wants to do through them. (EGO = "Exalting God Only," instead of "Edging God Out" [Blanchard and Hodges, *Lead Like Jesus*])

14. Servant-stewards demonstrate a biblical understanding of Christ as the center. Their focus is on Christ and not on self.

Their use of the personal pronoun "I" points to the supremacy of Christ and not to their own personal success or achievements.

15. Servant-stewards demonstrate a positive attitude, focusing on what God is providing, rather than on what is not available.

Gratitude is evident in their lives. They demonstrate a thankfulness to God for what He is doing—to Him alone *be honor and glory forever and ever.*
(See numbers 10, 54)

1 Tim. 1:18
16. When an individual is named to a place of leadership, it should not be surprising to those who have known him.
(See number 12)

They have been tested. They are known and have given evidence of their capability.
Prophesies. Paul and others likely could see leadership qualities in Timothy from his earliest days as a young believer or as he was being set apart for ministry by the elders (1 Tim. 4:14, see also 1 Tim. 3:10; Titus 1:5-9)

1 Tim. 1:18-20
17. Servant-stewards do what is right because it is right.

Wage the good warfare. They are able to discern reality and are willing to proactively engage it.
(See numbers 56, 72)

1 Tim. 1:20
18. Servant-stewards recognize that not everyone can be rescued.

They are able to allow some people to go their separate way if these are insistent on following the wrong path.

Hymenaeus and Alexander, whom I have handed over

to Satan. (Later see how these verses relate to Titus 3, dealing with issues. More on Hymenaeus in 2 Tim. 2:17, 18.) These two vigorously pursued heretical teaching. (See also Titus 3:10-11)

19. Servant-stewards recognize the fact that anyone can fall unless they stay on the right path all the time.

They recognize their own vulnerability and are careful to protect the integrity of their testimony and ministry as they also help others to do the same.

1 Tim. 2:1-8

1 Tim. 2:2
20. Servant-stewards recognize and respect the authority of others over them.
(See numbers 42, 71)

Paul urged his readers to pray for the authorities, including secular leaders, over us. Pray for tranquility (peace) so that the gospel can flourish. Leaders should recognize that people under their authority are praying for tranquility. Leadership brings both responsibility and accountability to live a life of dignity (dignified, respectful of others).

21. Servant-stewards see their role of authority as a responsibility, not as a privilege.
(See numbers 3, 9, 25, 34, 63)

22. Servant-stewards take seriously their responsibility to live a life of dignity, treating others with proper respect.

Spiritual leaders see themselves as peers "in Christ" with those they lead. The leader is a fellow struggler who happens to be in a position of servanthood to others.

1 Tim. 2:9-15
Eve was deceived by the serpent, but Adam *knew* what he was doing when he took the fruit and ate... This emphasis addresses the issue of spiritual authority in the local church. The context is Paul writing to Timothy as he is establishing leadership in the local church. Women are not to have spiritual authority over men, specifically in the church. Since churches in the New Testament were household churches, then it also would stand that a woman should not have spiritual authority over a man in the local church because the man is to be the spiritual leader of his own household.

This does not apply to women in the workplace where some women will be supervisors over men.

1 Tim. 3:1-16
The role of a supervisor is not precisely the same as that of a pastor or deacon within a local church. We are, however, still of the church as individuals and the role of supervisor is often pastoral in the service of others. Therefore, all the requirements of leadership apply. As believers we must hold ourselves to the highest standards because we are servants of God.

1 Tim. 3:1-13
The requirements of both the overseer (*obispos*) and the servant (*diakonos*) apply to anyone who would aspire, desire, set his heart on being a leader. In v. 8 *likewise* reemphasizes what already has been stated about the overseer—same, same, but different.

Deacons (servants) are to be held to the same standard. (See note on Titus 1:5-9)

1 Tim. 3:2-3
Must be above reproach, of good reputation. How else can they deal with the difficult issues that arise? This includes both dealing with the issues concerning the people they lead and also being able to stand confidently when false accusations are made against them. This is also related to the *good conscience* mentioned in 1 Tim. 1:5, 19 and 2 Tim. 1:3.

23. **Servant-stewards have a clear understanding of their personal core values.**
    Their mind is already made up about ethical issues. They already know what they will or will not do. (See numbers 6, 17, 56, 72)

24. **Servant-stewards know when to engage and when not to engage.**

    They know when to speak up or confront and when to remain silent. They are not quarrelsome or argumentative. (See also numbers 7, 38; 1 Tim. 5:20)

25. **Servant-stewards do not bully the people they lead. Rather, they treat others with respect and gentleness.**
    (See numbers 9, 34)

1 Tim. 3:10
26. **Servant-stewards have no obvious or hidden vices or character flaws.**

    There is no evidence of hidden vices or character flaws. Although these might not be obvious in the public view, external evidences such as relationship problems or excessive personal stress could be symptomatic of underlying hidden flaws. If it appears that "something ain't right," it is probably because "something ain't right." (See also 1 Tim. 5:24-25)

They have been *tested*. They are known and have given evidence of their capability. (See number 16)

1 Tim. 3:12
27. **Servant-stewards are consistent in their personal integrity.**

They are the same person at home as at work. (See also 1 Tim. 3:4; numbers 52, 62, 70)

28. **Servant-stewards are also good judges of character.**
They are wise in choosing the company they keep and in the selection of others with whom they will work. (see numbers 41, 67)

1 Tim. 3:13
29. **Servant-stewards are respected by others.**
(See number 12)

1 Tim. 3:14-16
Godliness is how everyone in the church should conduct themselves, both at home and at work. The model is Jesus, God revealed in the flesh. Jesus modeled servant-stewardship (Phil.2:5-11; Mt.20:25-28; Jn.17:12)

1 Tim. 4:1-5
Spiritual leaders recognize false teaching. False doctrine comes from Satan. There are only two possibilities—Truth is of God, everything else is false and of Satan. There can be no middle ground. When anyone turns away from the truth and teaches false

doctrine in opposition to Scripture, believers who have been immersed in scriptural truth will recognize it immediately. The way to overcome false doctrine is to concentrate on teaching the truth, not to be consumed with disputing false doctrine.

30. Servant-stewards constantly put forth a godly standard for others to follow.

1 Tim. 4:6-10

31. Servant-stewards are lifelong learners. They recognize that godliness requires continual training.

In verse 6 ESV and NASB translate the Greek word *diakonos* as "servant;" KJV and NIV translate it as "minister." All the training and spiritual preparation of the servant-steward has been for the purpose of serving God. Training, however, is not a time-defined series of courses, it is a life-long challenge. Paul challenges Timothy to continue his training as he nourishes his character in godliness.

1 Tim. 4:10
Spiritual leaders recognize the eternal impact of what they teach. They stand on the eternal truth of Scripture. They teach out of the truth they are currently learning or have already learned, examined and tested. (see also 4:16)

1 Tim. 4:11-16
They take command when appropriate and/or necessary, establishing clear parameters for those they lead as they actively teach the truth.

Their authority is derived, not from age, but from the evidence of the Holy Spirit in their life. (See numbers 20 and 21 above.) Their lifestyle and teaching are consistent and in agreement with each other, not contradictory or hypocritical.

1 Tim. 4:12
32. Supervisors are chosen because others recognize the Spirit-given gift in them.

1 Tim. 4:14
33. Servant-stewards validate the gift in others.

...as Paul did for Timothy and Titus. Paul is not described as a "Barnabas," but he certainly seems like one in his writings to these two young leaders whom he encouraged and mentored.

Do not neglect the gift you have is a stewardship issue. They recognize the stewardship responsibility that comes with any gift from God—including spiritual gifts. (See number 7; also see 1 Tim. 1:18)

1 Tim. 5:1-16
34. Servant-stewards show genuine concern for the people they lead and provide appropriate help for them to flourish.
(see numbers 9, 25)

Be concerned for the people you are leading. Good leadership requires the ability to discern their real needs to provide intelligent help.

1 Tim. 5:17-18
35. Servant-stewards give honor and recognition for the good work of those they lead.
(This includes honoring age and experience.)

People need to be encouraged, recognized in some way for their hard work.

<u>1 Tim. 5:19-24</u>
36. Servant-stewards actively seek feedback from appropriate sources to evaluate the work of their direct reports, adding this to their own observations.

37. Servant-stewards make it easy for others to give honest feedback.

Do not allow yourself to condemn too quickly without confirming any accusations. Don't fall into the trap of a "knee-jerk" reaction that might not be warranted.

<u>1 Tim. 5:19-20</u>
38. Servant-stewards seek the correction of behaviors and not the destruction of individuals.
(see numbers 7, 24, 58, 63)

In confronting any failure or accused sin, the biblical mandate of *two or three witnesses* is to be applied. Be careful not to shame others unnecessarily, especially if they are older. Be sensitive to the timing, type and context of the confrontation. (See also Mt.18:15-20)

<u>1 Tim. 5:21</u>
39. Servant-stewards strive to be impartial as they make every effort to deal with people equitably.

Do nothing from partiality. Avoid the appearance and perception of inappropriate behavior. Avoid the appearance of any favoritism to others or personal entitlement above what is expected of others.

40. Servant-stewards lead out of *character* and not out of preferential relationships.

200

(Recognize that who you are is more important than who know or what you know.)

1 Tim. 5:22
41. Servant-stewards are careful in the selection and endorsement of new leaders.
(see numbers 28, 67)

Do not be hasty. Be careful in the selection of new leaders. Take appropriate steps, ask questions, examine carefully. Be aware of the responsibility that will be carried on in future generations, aware of the long-term implications of choosing poorly.

1 Tim. 6:1-2
42. Servant-stewards are respectful of those in authority over them.
(See also number 20, 71)

The best leaders are also good followers. (see also Titus 3:1) Continuing from 5:24-25, one way to show good deeds is to be respectful of those in authority, regardless of whether they are believers or not. Good leaders avoid discriminating against others who are not in agreement or do not hold the same beliefs. They also do not seek to profit personally from their personal relationships with those who are in authority over them.

Two perspectives on 1 Tim. 6:2:
> 1) If the one in authority is a believer, do not be disrespectful—show respect, because they are a believer.
> 2) Don't take advantage of the fact that one in authority is also a believer—show proper respect.

1 Tim. 6:3-10

43. Servant-stewards are more concerned with godly living than with worldly gain.

Two adjectives to describe the leader:
1) *Godliness.* (1 Tim. 6:6) This is a heart issue, related to how *gain* is defined. Godliness is not a means for physical gain. Spiritual leaders understand that *to live is Christ* (Phi 1:21), because their identity is in Him. Their desire is to find gain in Christ rather than in monetary riches. They see the *great gain* as Christ himself.

2) *Contentment.* (1 Tim. 6:6-8) Good contentment does not lead to idleness, but to a good ambition for the right things, in the right way with the right motive. Such inner contentment comes from inner strength, strength of character. With this inner strength, the leader can then fight the good fight.

Unhealthy Craving for controversy (1 Tim. 6:4). Diseased appetite, conceit, envy, covetousness all lead to quarrels and dissension. Some people are never satisfied, they never feel content and so become contentious, seeming to always be in a fight for more riches, more power, more recognition. How many fights grow out of disagreements over money! (Mt. 6:33, priorities)

44. Servant-stewards possess an inner strength of contentment with what God has provided them.

At the same time, they are not content to sit idly by and ignore needs in the world around them. e.g., They are not content with the lostness of the world. They are content with God as the source of the resources. (See also numbers 10, 15)

1 Tim. 6:11-20

45. Servant-stewards choose their battles, then fight their battles well.

Fight the good fight of (with) *faith* and with a good conscience. Fighting the good fight also implies fighting the right fight, fighting appropriately and with maturity, using the right resources—in short, doing what is right because it is right. (See also Titus 2:15)

2 Timothy

2 Tim. 1:1-2
Grace, mercy and peace (are) *from God.* The leader needs grace and mercy that lead to peace.
(See number 77)

2 Tim. 1:3
Paul again mentions his clear conscience. (1 Tim. 1:5, 19).

2 Tim. 1:4-6
46. Servant-stewards build genuine, caring relationships with the people they lead.

I remember your tears... Paul was very familiar with Timothy's personal life—his family, his history and his giftedness. As a leader, he was involved with his followers—emotionally, spiritually and personally. He recognized and affirmed that God had given Timothy a special gift for ministry.
He did not learn these things by talking but by engaging in dialogue and getting to know Timothy and his family.

47. Servant-stewards affirm the faith of others and the power of the Holy Spirit at work in them.

2 Tim. 1:7
48. Servant-stewards encourage others to work from their giftedness with confidence.

The best leaders can act with appropriate confidence because they operate *not out of fear* or timidity, but with *self-control* and love that draws on the power of the Holy Spirit at work in them.

2 Tim. 1:12-14

49. Servant-stewards act with appropriate confidence giving evidence of the fruit of the Spirit in every aspect of their daily lives.

ESV translates 1:12 *what has been entrusted to me*; ASV, KJV and NIV translate it *that which I have committed* (entrusted or given) *to Him.* Whether it is trusting God with what we bring him, or trusting him to lead as we steward what he has provided, either way, the focus is on *God* as the one who is able to take care of everything related to the stewardship responsibilities he has assigned to his servants. Paul also reminds Timothy that he has preached this message consistently and constantly and that Timothy should follow the same pattern (1:13).

2 Tim. 1:15-18
Paul drew examples from past experience to share teachable moments with his mentees. He consistently followed a pattern of sound teaching, sharing from personal experience examples of how to deal with both opposition and support from others. *All who are in Asia turned away from me...* Although he chose good people to join his team, some of those chosen later turned away from the faith.

2 Tim. 2:1- 2

50. Servant-stewards know they cannot do the job by themselves. They recognize their need for the Holy Spirit and value the help of others.
(See numbers 5, 13)

2 Tim. 2:2 provides the key principle of spiritual leadership. Verse 2 is grounded in verse 1. The leader must firm and secure in their own faith first. The best leaders draw confidence from and are strengthened by the grace of Christ Jesus at work in them. *Faithful men*

who will be able to teach others also... With the help of the Holy Spirit, the best leaders select good people, then teach as they also teach these to teach still others. (Waylon Moore—look for **F A T** people: Those chosen must be **F**aithful, **A**vailable and **T**eachable.) Although it might be "easier" to do it alone, the best leaders recognize the opportunity to multiply themselves through others, thus accomplishing in the long run far more than could have been accomplished alone.

51. Servant-stewards gather the right people to join them in the task.

2 Tim. 2:2
What you have heard from me in the presence of many witnesses... Timothy had traveled with Paul and heard him speak in many places before many people. Paul reminded Timothy that he had consistently shared the same message many times before many witnesses and that his followers were to share this same message with still others (see also 2 Tim. 1:13 above). In his letter to the Philippians he says much the same thing, adding that he practiced what he preached and encouraged others to follow the example of both his teaching and his practice: *"What you have learned and received and heard and seen in me— practice these things."* (Php. 4:9)

52. Servant-stewards are consistent in the message they communicate.
(2 Tim. 1:13; 2:2; 3:10-11)
(see number 27, 62, 70)

2 Tim. 2:3-13
53. Servant-stewards are willing to "get their hands dirty," sharing in the work with those they lead.
(see number 4)

Paul shared in the work with his followers. He was
willing to get his hands dirty. He was willing to suffer
for the right reasons—that is, for the sake of the gospel.

1 Tim. 2:8-9
**54. Their priority is not on policies, but rather on
the proclamation of the gospel.**
(see number 11)

Keep in mind that Paul was writing to Timothy from
prison where he was *bound with chains* because of his
commitment to share the gospel openly in a hostile
environment. Servant-stewards are firm in their faith
and their focus is on the priority of sharing the gospel.
They are willing to endure hardships for the sake of the
gospel, so that still others will come to faith. Paul also
seemed to offer a strong affirmation of Timothy's
ability to also do what was right: *The Lord will give
you understanding in everything.* (2 Tim. 2:7)

Receive - 2 Tim. 2:6. The worker is worthy of his
wages. We do not have to feel guilty for receiving an
appropriate income.
Reflect – 2 Tim. 2:8. The servant-steward should
spend time reflecting on what he has been taught,
applying lessons from the past.
Remember – 2 Tim. 2:8. Paul constantly reminded his
followers to remember the priority of the gospel.
Remind – 2 Tim. 2:14. He charged Timothy to also
continually remind others of this priority.
(see also Titus 3:1-7)

2 Tim. 2:14-19
**55. Servant-stewards coach, give advice or counsel,
and then allow the Lord to do the work.**

56. Servant-stewards inspire confidence in others to do what is right.
(see numbers 17, 72)

Not to quarrel about words... Many, perhaps most arguments are over the meaning of words and the underlying motivation from which they emerge. Idle words can lead to hurt feelings. All too often we will spend time talking **about issues** instead of talking **to the person**. Paul warns Timothy how easy it can be for "idle talk" coming from wrong motives and wrong thinking can lead to discord, destruction and heresy. *Hymenaeus and Philetus* are presented as examples of how getting off course with words that are not edifying can ultimately lead to a break in fellowship that damages the body of Christ.

The servant-steward must be prepared to confront people with issues rather than simply discussing the issues apart from the people.

2 Tim. 2:20-21
57. Servant-stewards continually seek to grow in their own faith and self-awareness of their strengths and liabilities.

The smallest of flaws can become chinks in the spiritual armor that can impede the effective leadership of the servant-steward. As a leader, you must constantly take your own spiritual temperature, taking inventory of the things in your life that might become stumbling blocks or hindrances for your own spiritual growth.

2 Tim. 2:22-26; 3:1-9

58. Servant-stewards are willing to confront appropriately and in a timely manner when necessary, for both the good of the individual as well as the good of the body.

Appropriately includes a kind, loving and gentle spirit with strong, firm conviction.
(see numbers 3, 9, 63)

Youthful passions relates to immaturity, self-centeredness. Misplaced passion can become harmful to others. Passion is often affirmed as a strong value in young leaders. Passion is only valuable if it is focused on the right priorities. Arguments or quarrels become senseless when righteousness, faith, love, peace and a pure heart are taken out of the conversation.

[Leadership hint: Whenever anyone is displaying what they might call "righteous indignation" or justified anger, ask, "Help me to understand—What aspect of the fruit of the Spirit are you demonstrating right now?" (Gal.5:22)]

The best leaders are able to "take the heat and still be sweet." Leaders must endure verbal attacks that often come unexpectedly and from unexpected people. You must not allow yourself to become embittered or resentful toward those who oppose you, but rather you must *patiently endure* the attacks. (2 Tim. 2:24) You should not become embroiled in a battle of words. At times this might mean enduring in silence. At other times it will require a large measure of patience to gently and lovingly deal with the offender.

The purpose of corrective action is not to punish, but to *correct* and be redemptive. Being *kind* and *not quarrelsome* enables you as a leader to teach those you are leading. There is no need to be mean if you already have the authority and power. (2 Tim. 2:24-26; Titus 3:10-11).

Do you want to make a point or make a difference? Effective supervisors are able to make a point with gentle firmness in such a way as to make a difference in the individual's life, even if it must lead to separation and helping the individual to move on to another place or with other employment.

Corrective action should take place at the earliest opportunity to help individuals avoid the *snare* (trap) *of the devil* and being used by him. (2 Tim. 2:26). *Repentance* means a change of heart. Early corrective action will help some individuals see the error of their unacceptable behavior and lead them to repentance and corrected behavior.

2 Tim. 3:1-9
59. **Servant-stewards hold themselves to a high standard, taking every precaution to avoid even the appearance of evil.**
(see number 68)

Effective spiritual leaders are careful not to give even the appearance of evil. *Avoid such people* today can also be an admonition to avoid entertaining certain visual images in one's home. Viewing pornography is the most common form of associating with people who are *lovers of self, lovers of money, proud, arrogant, abusive, disobedient to their parents, ungrateful, unholy, heartless, unappeasable, slanderous, without self-control, brutal, not loving good, treacherous, reckless, swollen with conceit, lovers of pleasure rather than lovers of God, having the appearance of godliness, but denying its power.* (2 Tim. 3:2-5)

With the massive proliferation and easy access of pornography, even the best of spiritual leaders today must be on the alert to *avoid such people* in person or in images.

2 Tim. 3:10-11

60. Servant-stewards are transparent about their personal lives and vulnerabilities, allowing their followers the opportunity to know them.

This is a key passage for understanding the role of servant-steward. Paul emphasizes to Timothy again, "You know me." How important it is for those who follow to **know** their leader. Trust is built from knowing the person. This requires transparency on the part of the leader which also makes his leadership predictable—in a good way. It is easier to trust a leader that is known than one who is aloof. Paul also set himself as an example, a model and a mentor. He gave God the credit for giving him the grace and strength to pass through difficult times of persecution. Patience, love, steadfastness and suffering characterize Paul's teaching, his personal conduct, his life goals, and his personal faith. In dealing with difficult people, you must exercise patience that comes from love for the people you lead.

61. Servant-stewards build trust by showing their trustworthiness.

62. Servant-stewards are persons of integrity. Their daily lives (public and private) are consistent with their public teaching.
(see numbers 27, 52, 70)

63. Servant-stewards show patience and love when it is necessary to correct others.
(See numbers 3, 9, 58)

2 Tim. 3:12-13
64. Servant-stewards recognize that they will face opposition/persecution if they are living a godly life.

Paul affirmed that opposition and persecution were to be expected because of his having led a godly life. *All who desire to live a godly life in Christ Jesus will be persecuted.* In fact, he affirmed that evil would continue to increase from bad to worse. Servant-stewards who apply these principles in the workplace can expect to face opposition and persecution.

2 Tim. 3:14-4:8
65. Servant-stewards know how to correctly use Scripture to equip themselves and others for effective ministry.

Spiritual leaders do not speak from their own authority, but from an ascribed authority. Paul again affirms his confidence, not in himself, but with a confidence that grows from his trust in God. The opposite of fear is trust. Paul's message to the young leader was that he should stay true to the biblical message in spite of the fact that others might offer a popularized version of the gospel. In this current age when many people are seeking a church they like, some leaders will try to make the message of the Bible culturally relevant, but God's Word is already relevant. *Preach the word,* Paul instructed, because the Word of God is a powerful tool for countering false doctrine. Let the Word speak for itself. The best tool for defending the Word is the Word itself.

66. Servant-stewards are careful about how and when to use Scripture when applying corrective action, while maintaining a strong biblical foundation for all they do.
(see number 58)

Although you might not quote Scripture when dealing with administrative actions, you will want to maintain a strong biblical foundation for all you do. If confronted with the question, "Who are you to speak to me this way?" you can answer, "I am no one, but this is God's Word and I stand on its authority." (See also Titus 1:1-4; 1:9; 2:5; 2:1; 2:10)

2 Tim. 4:5
This one verse provides an outline for the evaluation of servant-stewards. Just four open-ended questions. Simple. To the point. Focused on growing as a leader.

Is this person:
1) Clear-headed? (*sober-minded*, not carried away by emotion, steady)
2) Able to endure hardships or criticism? (Velcro-Teflon; does criticism or opposition seem to stick or can they allow it to slide off and not affect their attitude negatively)
3) Doing the work of an evangelist? (personal involvement in making disciples, involved in Main Thing, work focused on seeing fruit for the Kingdom)
4) Fulfilling their ministry? (doing the job they are assigned to do and using their time wisely)

(See "The Servant-Steward Coaching Guide" with expanded coaching questions to stimulate dialogue in a supervisory coaching dialogue in business or ministry settings.)

2 Tim. 4:9-18

67. Servant-stewards prepare for succession.
(See numbers 28, 41)

Several times Paul reminded Timothy of the younger leader's upbringing, his training, his preparation for leadership. Now Paul is ready to pass the baton to the next generation. As he recognizes he is coming to the end of his assignment, he lists several people who are already active in the ministry, multiplying his efforts to impact many more places with the gospel. He also acknowledges a few who started out with him and later abandoned the ministry. Paul gives recognition to Mark as an example of one who failed to complete his first assignment with Paul (Acts 12:25; 13:13; 15:37-38) but was given a second chance and became effective.

Paul's passion was not in opposition to those who opposed him. His passion was in the positive proclamation of the whole gospel. (See numbers 10, 15, 54)

Titus

Introduction to Titus (Integrity)
"Paul expected the gospel, even in Crete, to produce
real godliness in everyday life. . . .(He) describes
proper leadership (Titus 1:5–9), proper handling of
error (Titus 1:10–16; 3:9–11), proper Christian living
(Titus 2:1–10; 3:1–2), and the gospel as the source of
godliness (Titus 2:11–14; 3:3–7)."
(from "Introduction to Titus," *ESV Bible*, Crossway.)

Titus 1:1-4
Paul presented his "bonafides," establishing the
spiritual authority for the instructions he would give
Titus in the present letter. Although he was not one of
the original twelve, he affirmed his own apostleship
based on his calling to share the Good News (preaching
the gospel) with the non-Jewish world. Having
declared the basis from which his spiritual authority
derived, he did not need to belabor it, although he
reemphasized several times in the letter that his
instructions are solidly rooted in the foundation of the
gospel and the Word of God (Titus 1:9; 2:5; 2:1; 2:10).
(See numbers 2, 65, 66)

Titus 1:5
**68. Servant-stewards must hold themselves to
higher standards of conduct, regardless of
their title or position.**
(See number 59)

The issue of appointing leaders can be a thorny one.
Paul instructed Titus to appoint elders for the local
churches in each town of Crete. With the criteria for
spiritual leadership clearly outlined, the selection of
such leaders should not be controversial.
(see also 1 Tim. 1:18; 3:10).
(See numbers 5, 12, 16, 29)

Titus 1:5-9
69. **Servant-stewards demonstrate their integrity by practicing at home what they teach in public.**
(see numbers 52, 62,)

In writing to Timothy and Titus, Paul used specific words to describe individuals with distinct ministries: *episkopos* – bishop or overseer (Titus 1:7; 1 Tim. 3:2). The only other time Paul used this term was in addressing the "overseers" and deacons at Philippi (Php 1:1).

presbyteros – elder (1 Tim. 5:17; 5:19; Titus 1:5). This word is also translated "older" referring to older men and older women in the church (1 Tim. 5:1; 5:2).
diakonos/ diakoneō – deacon or servant (1 Tim. 3:8; 3:12; 4:6; 1 Tim3:10; 3:13; 2 Tim. 1:18)
The word *diakonia* is often translated as "ministry" or "service" (1 Tim. 1:12; 2 Tim. 4:5; 4:11).

The lines of distinctions and definitions of roles between different levels of leadership have become somewhat blurred in our current setting. There do, however, seem to be differences of gifting, calling and responsibilities assigned to each of the three categories. In selecting under-leaders, the servant-steward should look for people who are already recognized by others for their good character. (See number 16)

Transparency in the leader is essential. A person of good character will have no secret vices or skeletons in a closet to hide. Their good character (1:7) will be biblically based (1:9), thus their doing will grow out of their being.

The most effective leaders are also good stewards of their family responsibilities. This requires that the leader must be faithful to lead their own family in the instruction of the Word. The support of the family for the servant-steward's leadership role is also important.

Titus 1:10-16; 2:1
This tirade against the Cretans seems harsh and highly prejudicial. Titus 1:10-16 is contrasted by the passages surrounding it, 1:5-9 and 2:1-14. The local culture, Cretans, accepted as normal certain behaviors that are unacceptable for followers of Jesus Christ.

Paul warned Titus not to allow cultural norms to define acceptable behavior. Certain practices that are considered acceptable in an unredeemed culture are not acceptable in a redeemed culture. As a spiritual leader, Titus was to lead others to be willing to go against culture wherever the gospel confronts it. In reality, it is the gospel that confronts the culture. The leader must, therefore, *teach what accords with sound doctrine,* stand firmly on biblical principles, and allow the gospel to do its work *that the word of God may not be reviled* (Titus 2:5). As the leader teaches sound biblical doctrine, the people will confront their own culture where the gospel confronts it.

Titus 2:1-14
The Bible provides a solid standard for acceptable behavior. Any leader in any organization could benefit from this leadership manual. The problem with most modern leadership literature is its attempt to teach leaders to practice certain principles without changing the underlying beliefs required to support the new behaviors. In effect, modern leadership theory encourages the leader to act like a Christian without having to live like one. The relevancy of all that Paul

wrote to Timothy and Titus proves the value of
absolute Truth. (see numbers 10, 11)

Titus 2:7-8
**70. Servant-stewards are persons of integrity,
providing a model for others in their teaching
and their practice.**
(see numbers 27, 52, 62)

At least five times Paul emphasizes the need for people
to exercise self-control—older men (Titus 2:2), older
women (Titus 2:3), younger women (Titus 2:5),
younger men (Titus 2:6), all of us (Titus 2:12) should
learn to control our behaviors and not allow our
behaviors to control us. Self-control is one aspect or
evidence of the fruit of the Spirit (Gal 5:22-23). Self-
discipline is the ability to control one's own behavior
and not allow circumstances or one's own behavior to
control him. Paul instructed Titus to teach everyone to
exercise self-control. The older man might have more
experience, but his passion might be waning, so he
needs to control how much advice he offers. The
younger man might have all the passion, but still lacks
experience, so he might need to control how bullishly
he presses on a "new" idea that might not be so new
after all.

"We who lived in the concentration camps can
remember the men who walked through the huts
comforting others, giving away their last piece of
bread. They may have been few in number, but they
offer sufficient proof that everything can be taken from
a man but one thing: The last of his freedoms – to
choose one's attitude in any given set of circumstances,
to choose one's own way."
(Victor Frankl, *Man's Search for Meaning*)

Titus 2:9-10; 3:1-7
71. Servant-stewards are respectful and submissive to those in authority over them.
(see number 20, 42)

The best leaders are also good followers, even when they might not be in total agreement with their superiors. (1 Tim. 6:1-2) When they are treated unfairly, their response is not argumentative. They can be loyal to their leaders, recognizing that they are ultimately serving God by honoring Him and actively living according to the principles in His Word.

Titus 3:1-7
There are times when the leader must remind his followers that we all are under authority (see numbers 20, 42, 71). The leader should never assume that people know what is expected of them. At the same time, policies should not be so restrictive that the individual's creativity is squashed. Paul used precise language to communicate his expectations clearly in writing to Timothy and Titus.

Titus 2:15
At the same time, the best leaders are willing to stand up for what is right. They can confront bad behavior in love. They can condemn the guilty act without condemning the actor. They can assign guilt without forcing shame. Paul instructed Titus to stand on the firm foundation of the gospel and follow the example of Jesus Christ, in spite of his youthfulness or lack of status. As a leader, he was to speak with all the authority of Scripture backing him up.

Titus 2:15-3:9
72. Servant-stewards stand up for what is right, even when they stand alone.
(see numbers 6, 17, 56)

The best leaders learn to exercise good judgment based on values. They are consistent, while they also are not driven by policy. They recognize the purpose of policy is to help people to be more productive and successful in their assignments while also helping them to contribute to fulfilling the corporate vision. They can discern when to maintain and adhere to a policy, when to make exceptions, and when it is time to change a policy. The best leaders know the limits within which they can make exceptions and when to appeal to the next level of authority.

At the same time, the best leaders are willing to stand up for what is right. They can confront bad behavior in love. They can condemn the guilty act without condemning the actor. They can assign guilt without forcing shame. Paul instructed Titus to stand on the firm foundation of the gospel and follow the example of Jesus Christ, in spite of his youthfulness or lack of status. As a leader, he was to speak with all the authority of Scripture backing him up.

They also understand the reality of limited resources and the need for consistency in administering these equitably, both for the good of the organization and for the good of the people they lead. The point of these instructions was to help the people do well and succeed (Titus 3:8). Clear communication of expectations also tells the people how they will know when they have succeeded in their work by establishing a "plumb line" of expected acceptable behaviors.

Titus 3:8
73. Servant-stewards want their people to succeed.

Titus 3:9

74. Servant-stewards communicate clear expectations, then offer help to meet these.

Several times, Paul warns both Timothy and Titus to avoid getting caught up in pointless quarrels, or arguments over issues (1 Tim. 6:20; 2 Tim. 2:16; Titus 3:2; 3:9). He described such quarrels as *irreverent babble* (1 Tim. 6:20) or *foolish controversies.* (Titus 3:9) Instead, he insisted that we are to show *perfect courtesy toward all people.* (Titus 3:2) Even when dealing with difficult people, the best leaders are courteous and respectful in their demeanor. If they know you love them and want the best for them, there is no limit to where people will follow. (1 Tim. 1:5-7; 2 Tim1:7; numbers 3, 9, 58, 63) Such love and respect are also a prerequisite to successful corrective action.

Titus 3:10-11 (see also 2 Tim. 2:24-26)

75. Servant-stewards recognize that some people need to go and are willing to make the hard decisions when necessary.
(see number 18)

Corrective action = confronting in love. When an individual's behavior is unacceptable, the loving thing to do is to confront with love, respect and consideration for the person (Titus 3:1). The purpose of a first warning is to help the person correct their unacceptable behavior. As difficult as it is to receive a warning, if they know you love them and want them to succeed, there is better hope for the counsel and instruction to be well-taken. If, however, the counsel or instruction is not well-taken and the person continues in the unacceptable behavior, a second, stronger warning is in order. Paul instructed that there was to be no third warning. This "three strikes and you are out" approach requires:

1) Close communication between the leader and the follower. The leader cannot correct behaviors of which he is unaware. This also requires talking *to* people and not *about* them.

2) Immediate confrontation. As soon as the unacceptable behavior is observed or reported, it should be confronted. The longer the behavior goes without confrontation, the more ingrained it will become and the more difficult to correct. Failure to confront becomes a tacit approval of the unacceptable behavior.

3) Clear communication of the leader's sincere desire for the individual to succeed. This includes the need for the leader to offer appropriate assistance to help the individual change the behavior.

4) Clear communication of expectations. The leader should outline clearly what the unacceptable behavior is and what corrected, acceptable behavior will look like. This will also prescribe what success should look like.

5) Clear communication of the consequences that will follow failure to correct the behavior.

6) Clear communication of a timeline within which the correction must take place.

7) Firm commitment on the part of the leader to follow up:
    a) with praise, if the behavior is corrected.
    b) with appropriate action if the behavior is not corrected.
        i) second warning
        ii) separation

Titus 3:12
Paul was aware of many other people who could be available as helpful resource people. He made some

specific suggestions of people who could be helpful to him, and he also mentioned the help he was sending to Titus.

Titus 3:13-14
Paul was also aware of the needs of his colleagues. He commented on Timothy's health (1 Tim. 5:23) and was concerned about the needs for Zenas and Apollos *see that they lack nothing* (3:13). Paul instructed Titus to encourage the people to do good works, *so that* they can be fruitful. (3:8, 14) Addressing human needs is good. God's people should help meet the pressing needs of others around them, *so that* they can be fruitful (*not be unfruitful* = be fruitful). God's people should be alert to the needs of others around them and ready *to help in cases of urgent need.* (3:14)

76. Servant-stewards stay in touch with the needs of their followers and are ready to suggest helpful resources when appropriate.

Titus 3:15
77. Servant-stewards recognize their own need for grace and extend grace to others as they exercise their responsibilities.
(see number 13)

Grace. Paul started all three letters to Timothy and Titus with a blessing of *grace and peace* and he ends them with a closing *grace to you all.* The leader needs grace and he also needs to grant grace to those he leads.

APPENDIX

(Some of the resources in the Appendix are available as downloadable forms at:
www.MyLEAD360.com/free-resources.html.)

Principles and Characteristics of the Servant-Steward

The Character and Characteristics of Effective Supervisors
Based on Paul's Letters to Timothy and Titus

1. **Servant-stewards see their role as more than a job—it is a calling. (1 Tim. 1:1; Titus 1:4)**
   - Servant-stewards understand their stewardship responsibility that comes from God by faith. (1 Tim. 1:3-4; 4:14)
   - Servant-stewards should be chosen based on clear evidence of God's call in their lives. (1 Tim. 1:12-17)
   - Servant-stewards are chosen because others recognize the Spirit-given gift in them. (1 Tim. 4:14)
   - When an individual is named to a place of leadership, it should not be surprising to those who have known him. (1 Tim. 1:18; 1 Tim. 3:10; Titus 1:5-9)
   - Servant-stewards are respected by others. (1 Tim. 3:13)

2. **Servant-stewards are persons of integrity, providing a model for others in their teaching and their practice. (Titus 2:7-8)**
   - Servant-stewards have no obvious or hidden vices or character flaws. (1 Tim. 4:2-3)
   - Servant-stewards are persons of integrity. Their daily lives (public and private) are consistent with their public teaching. (2 Tim. 3:10-11)
   - Servant-stewards demonstrate their integrity by practicing at home what they teach in public. (1 Tim. 3:11-12; Titus 1:5-9)
   - Servant-stewards are consistent in the message they communicate. (2 Tim. 1:13; 2:2; 3:10-11)
   - Servant-stewards constantly put forth a godly standard for others to follow. (1 Tim. 4:1-5)

- Servant-stewards hold themselves to a high standard of conduct, regardless of their title or position, taking every precaution to avoid even the appearance of evil. (2 Tim. 3:1-9; Titus 1:5; 1 Tim. 1:18; 3:10)
- Servant-stewards lead out of *character* and not out of preferential relationships. (1 Tim. 5:21)

3. **Servant-stewards have an observably close walk with the Lord. (1 Tim. 1:2-4)**
   - Servant-stewards act with appropriate confidence giving evidence of the fruit of the Spirit in every aspect of their daily lives. (2 Tim. 1:7)
   - Servant-stewards demonstrate a biblical understanding of Christ as the center. Their focus is on Christ and not on self. (1 Tim. 1:16-17)
   - Servant-stewards continually seek to grow in their own faith and self-awareness of their strengths and liabilities. (2 Tim. 2:20-21)

4. **Servant-stewards are blatantly biblical in the way they define and apply any authority. (1 Tim. 1:1; 2 Tim. 3:14-4:8)**
   - Servant-stewards know how to correctly use Scripture to equip themselves and others for effective ministry. (2 Tim. 3:14-4:8)
   - Servant-stewards are careful about how and when to use Scripture when applying corrective action, while maintaining a strong biblical foundation for all they do. (2 Tim. 2:22-26; 3:1-9; 3:14-4:8)

5. **Servant-stewards demonstrate the power of the presence of the Spirit in their demeanor, not "lording it over others." (1 Tim. 1:1-4)**
   - Servant-stewards demonstrate a genuine love for the people they lead. (1 Tim. 1:5-7)
   - Servant-stewards see their role of authority as a responsibility, not as a privilege. (1 Tim. 2:2)

- Servant-stewards do not bully the people they lead. (1 Tim. 4:2-3)
- Servant-stewards take seriously their responsibility to live a life of dignity, treating others with proper respect. (1 Tim. 2:2)
- Servant-stewards show genuine concern for the people they lead and provide appropriate help for them to flourish. (1 Tim. 5:1-16)
- Servant-stewards build genuine, caring relationships with the people they lead. (2 Tim. 1:4-6)
- Servant-stewards are transparent about their personal lives and vulnerabilities, allowing their followers the opportunity to know them. (2 Tim. 3:10-11)

6. Servant-stewards know how to confront appropriately. (1 Tim. 1:3-4)

- Servant-stewards know when to engage and when not to engage. (1 Tim. 4:2-3; 1 Tim. 5:20)
- Servant-stewards choose their battles, then fight their battles well. (1 Tim. 6:11-20)
- Servant-stewards are willing to confront appropriately and in a timely manner when necessary, for both the good of the individual as well as the good of the body. (2 Tim. 2:22-26; 3:1-9)
- Servant-stewards seek the correction of behaviors and not the destruction of individuals (1 Tim. 5:20)
- Servant-stewards show patience and love when it is necessary to correct others. (2 Tim. 3:10-11)
- Servant-stewards recognize the fact that anyone can fall unless they stay on the right path all the time. (1 Tim. 1:20)
- Servant-stewards recognize that not everyone can be rescued. (2 Tim. 2:17, 18; Titus 3:10-11)
- Servant-stewards are willing to make the hard decisions when necessary and at the appropriate time. (Titus 3:10-11; 2 Tim. 2:24-26)

7. **Servant-stewards are player-coaches. (1 Tim. 1:2)**
   - Servant-stewards recognize, respect and submit to the authority of others over them. (1 Tim. 2:2; 1 Tim. 6:1-2; Titus 2:9-10)
   - Servant-stewards are willing to "get their hands dirty," sharing in the work with those they lead. (2 Tim. 2:3-13)
   - Servant-stewards know they cannot do the job by themselves. They recognize their need for the Holy Spirit and value the help of others. (2 Tim. 2:1- 2)
   - Servant-stewards are lifelong learners. They recognize that godliness requires continual training. (1 Tim. 4:10, 16)

8. **Servant-stewards build trust by showing their trustworthiness. (2 Tim. 3:10-11)**
   - Servant-stewards demonstrate their trustworthiness to make good decisions based on knowing right from wrong. (1 Tim. 1:2-4)
   - Servant-stewards do what is right because it is right. (1 Tim. 1:18-20)
   - Servant-stewards stand up for what is right, even when they stand alone. (Titus 2:15)
   - Servant-stewards recognize that they will face opposition/persecution if they are living a godly life. (2 Tim. 3:12-13)
   - Servant-stewards have a clear understanding of their personal core values. (1 Tim. 4:2-3)
   - Servant-stewards inspire confidence in others to do what is right. (2 Tim. 2:3-13)

9. **Servant-stewards focus on positive goals. (1 Tim. 1:8-10)**
   - Servant-stewards demonstrate a positive attitude, focusing on what God is providing, rather than on what is not available. (1 Tim. 1:16-17)
   - Servant-stewards are more concerned with godly living than with worldly gain. (1 Tim. 6:3-10)

- Servant-stewards possess an inner strength of contentment with what God has provided them. (1 Tim. 6:3-10)

10. Servant-stewards recognize their need for the grace of God (mercy) as the basis for their success. (1 Tim. 1:12-17)

- Servant-stewards recognize their own need for grace and extend grace to others as they exercise their responsibilities. (Titus 3:15)
- Servant-stewards coach, give advice or counsel and then allow the Lord to do the work. (2 Tim. 2:8-9)

11. Servant-stewards prepare for succession. (2 Tim. 4:9-18)

- Servant-stewards are careful in the selection and endorsement of new leaders. (1 Tim. 5:22)
- Servant-stewards are good judges of character. (1 Tim. 3:12)
- Servant-stewards gather the right people to join them in the task. (2 Tim. 2:1- 2)

12. Servant-stewards give honor and recognition for the good work of those they lead. (1 Tim. 5:17-18)

- Servant-stewards communicate clear expectations, and then offer help to meet these. (Titus 3:8-9)
- Servant-stewards want their people to succeed. (Titus 3:8-9)
- Servant-stewards validate the gift in others. (1 Tim. 4:14)
- Servant-stewards affirm the faith of others and the power of the Holy Spirit at work in them. (2 Tim. 1:4-6)
- Servant-stewards encourage others to work from their giftedness with confidence. (2 Tim. 1:4-6)
- Servant-stewards actively seek feedback from appropriate sources to evaluate the work of their

direct reports, adding this to their own observations. (1 Tim. 5:19-24)

- Servant-stewards make it easy for others to give honest feedback. (1 Tim. 5:19-24)
- Servant-stewards strive to be impartial as they make every effort to deal with people equitably. (1 Tim. 5:21)
- Servant-stewards stay in touch with the needs of their followers and are ready to suggest helpful resources when appropriate. (Titus 3:13-14)

13. Servant-stewards build a culture of people who are not obsessed by the law or policies, but who see the practicality of *principles* which underlie the law. (1 Tim. 1:8-10; Titus 2:1-14; 3:9)

- Their priority is not on policies, but rather on the proclamation of the gospel. (2 Tim. 2:3-13; Titus 3:1-7)

Your Personal User Manual

Instructions for Writing Your Personal User Manual

Now that you have a better understanding of yourself and how you view others, use the outline below to write your own "User Manual" to share with your supervisor and others with whom you relate in your work or ministry. Your reflections in these categories will help you and your colleagues better understand not just who you are, but how to engage with you most productively.

We suggest organizing your thoughts with no more than four or five bullet points under each category and keep your outline to no more than one page in length. Be sure to include information you consider most important from your Grip-Birkman or Birkman reports to describe your personality, strengths, values, and workplace desires.

As you outline your manual, look back over your reports and consider these questions:

- Which activities energize me and which deplete me?
- What are my unique abilities, and how do I maximize the time I spend expressing them?
- What do people misunderstand about me, and why?

Organize your personal "User Manual" using the following outline. Although several points may overlap between sections, try to remain concise and specific.

Personal User Manual for:

_____

Here is a summary of some of the most important things I have learned about myself and how you can help me to be my most productive self.

1. My Strengths and Gifts

2. What motivates me

3. How to best communicate with me

4. Things that may cause me stress

5. How to help me be effective

6. Biggest mistakes you can make with me

Covenant Worksheet

Covenanting is a process. It is a way through which we can agree together upon the specifics of your role in your current assignment. Together, we will negotiate this role. Together, we will change it as situations and needs change. Together, we will evaluate it. Please complete "Your Personal User Manual" from your Birkman and/or Leadership Grip report before continuing with this worksheet.

In establishing our covenant, please be ready to discuss the following questions:

1. **Why** am I here?

2. What are my **expectations**?

3. What do l **need** from others at this time?

4. What **goals** need to be set in order to meet these personal needs?

5. What **tasks** should be developed to meet these personal goals?

6. How and when will we know we have accomplished my personal needs? (**evaluation**)

7. What work **needs** should I be addressing at this time?

8. What **goals** need to be set in order to meet these work needs?

9. What **tasks** should be developed to meet these work goals?

10. How and when will we know we have accomplished our work needs? (**evaluation**)

Sample Covenant Agreement Form

NAME:	
NEED TO BE ADDRESSED:	

GOAL 1:	DATE TO BE COMPLETED:
	Approximate Percentage of work time to complete this Goal: _____%

ACTIVITIES/ACTION PLAN:	Resources Needed:
1.	
1.	
3.	
4.	

Evaluation (What went well? What could have been improved? What next?):

The Servant-Steward Coaching Guide

(for business)
(Based on 2 Timothy 4:5)

The Apostle Paul provided a practical outline to help Timothy evaluate his own work: "As for you, always be sober-minded, endure suffering, do the work of an evangelist, fulfill your ministry." (2 Tim. 4:5) The following outline provides some suggested questions to provoke a coaching dialogue between supervisor and supervisee. **This list of questions is not exhaustive and not every question will apply in every situation.** These are offered to help start the conversation with the purpose of discovering how to help the individual continue growing in their assignment. The goal of this questionnaire is to provide an environment and opportunity for the coachee to do most of the talking. The coach should take an active listener role in order to learn about the coachee's attitudes, personalities, and expectations. Because of this, the actual dialogue may not cover all the categories or all of the questions listed here. Use your own judgement during the dialogue to determine the flow of the conversation. Both supervisor and supervisee should complete your initial scoring prior to the coaching dialogue. Scores are for the general category.

On a scale of 1 to 10 (1 low, 10 high), _at this time_, how are you doing in the following areas?

I) Sober-minded? (clear headed, not carried away by emotion, steady)
1. How is your family doing?
2. Describe any major decisions you had to make since our last evaluation dialogue?
3. Is there anything you would do differently if the same circumstances occurred in the future?
4. Do you ever feel overwhelmed by your responsibilities? If so, what are some of the causes?

5. Are you approaching this from your head or from your heart?
6. How long have you been thinking about this?
7. Are you focused on what's gone wrong or what's going right?

Score:_____ Comments:

II) Able to endure hardships or criticism? (enduring personal suffering)

1. Are you able to evaluate criticism to see how it applies without letting it affect you negatively?
2. What challenges have you encountered since our last coaching session?
3. Where are you facing the greatest opposition right now?
4. Tell me about any hard decisions you have had to make. How did that make you feel?
5. How have you dealt with any recent criticism or opposition?
6. What are you willing to do to improve this situation?
7. What's the emotional cost vs. the financial cost?
8. What challenges keep you awake at night?

Score:_____ Comments:

III) Doing the work of leading others? (succession planning)

1. Who are you leading right now?
2. Who do you see around you that might be a potential new leader?
3. If you were to be promoted or leave, who would take your place? Would they know how to do your job?

Score:_____ Comments:

IV) Fulfilling your assignment? (doing the assigned job
and using time wisely)
1. What are you most excited about in your work now?
   (What gets you up in the morning?)
2. What do you need to keep doing or do more to be
   effective in your assignment?
3. Is there anything you might need to stop doing to be
   more effective in your assignment?
4. Is there anything you are not doing that you ought to
   start doing?
5. What obstacles might be impeding your effectiveness in
   your job right now?
6. What potential crises do you see brewing in the future?
7. What two or three things do you need to focus on this
   year to help meet team or organizational goals?
8. What is the first step you need to take to reach your goal?
9. What plan do you need in order to achieve your new
   goals?
10. Is there anything you should delegate to someone else?
11. What help do need from me?

Score:_____ Comments:

How can I pray for you?

The Servant-Steward Coaching Guide

(for ministry)

(Based on 2 Timothy 4:5)

The Apostle Paul provided a practical outline to help Timothy evaluate his own work: "As for you, always be sober-minded, endure suffering, do the work of an evangelist, fulfill your ministry." (2 Tim. 4:5) The following outline provides some suggested questions to provoke a coaching dialogue between supervisor and supervisee.

This list of questions is not exhaustive and not every question will apply in every situation. These are offered to help start the conversation with the purpose of discovering how to help the individual continue growing in their assignment. The goal of this questionnaire is to provide an environment and opportunity for the coachee to do most of the talking. The coach should take an active listener role in order to learn about the coachee's attitudes, personalities, and expectations. Because of this, the actual dialogue may not cover all the categories or all of the questions listed here. Use your own judgement during the dialogue to determine the flow of the conversation. Both supervisor and supervisee should complete your initial scoring prior to the coaching dialogue. Scores are for the general category.

On a scale of 1 to 10 (1 low, 10 high), *at this time*, how are you doing in the following areas?

I) Sober-minded? (clear headed, not carried away by emotion, steady)
1. Tell me about your walk with the Lord.
2. How are you doing in caring for and ministering to your family?
3. Describe any major decisions you had to make since our last evaluation dialogue.

4. Is there anything you would do differently if the same circumstances occurred in the future?
5. Do you ever feel overwhelmed by your responsibilities? If so, what are some of the causes?
6. Are you approaching this from your head or from your heart?
7. How long have you been thinking about this?
8. Are you focused on what's going wrong or what's going right?

Score:_____ Comments:

II) Able to endure hardships or criticism? (enduring personal suffering)
1. Are you able to evaluate criticism to see how it applies without letting it affect you negatively?
2. What challenges have you encountered since our last coaching session?
3. Where are you facing the greatest opposition right now?
4. Tell me about any hard decisions you have had to make. How did that make you feel?
5. How have you dealt with any recent criticism or opposition?
6. What are you willing to do to improve this situation?
7. What's the emotional cost vs. the financial cost?
8. What challenges keep you awake at night?

Score:_____ Comments:

III) Doing the work of an evangelist? (making disciples, personal and catalytic involvement in evangelism, church planting and leadership training)
1. When was the last time you shared a significant portion of the gospel with a non-believer and called for a decision to follow Christ?
2. When was the last time you saw fruit from your witness?
3. Who are you discipling at this time? (How many Timothys are you training?)

4. When was the last time you took a new disciple out to do evangelism?
5. What help do you need in this area?

Score:_____ Comments:

IV) Fulfilling your ministry? (doing the assigned job and using time wisely)
1. What are you most excited about in your ministry now? (What gets you up in the morning?)
2. What do you need to keep doing or do more to be effective in your assignment?
3. Is there anything you might need to stop doing to be more effective in your assignment?
4. Is there anything you are not doing that you ought to start doing?
5. What obstacles might be impeding your effectiveness in your job right now?
6. What potential crises do you see brewing in the future?
7. What two or three things do you need to focus on this year to move the kingdom ahead?
8. Which of your core values does this goal express?
8. What is the first step you need to take to reach your goal?
9. What plan do you need in order to achieve your new goals?
10. Is there anything you should delegate to someone else?
11. What help do need from me?

Score:_____ Comments:

How can I pray for you?

Decision Tree for Prioritizing Your Tasks and Time

For each task, ask the following series of questions.

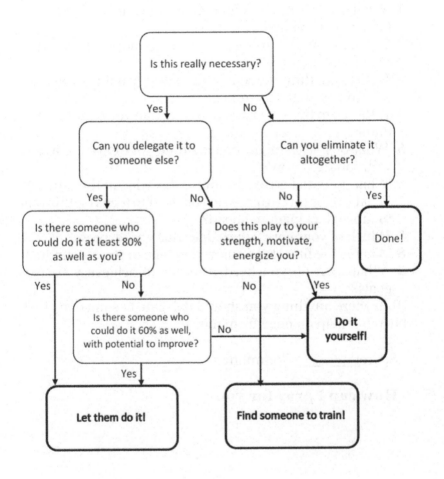

360 Degree Feedback and Evaluation

I. Personal Evaluation

(To be completed by each individual prior to the feedback dialogue.)

Before our feedback dialogue, please look over the goals you set for this year and write your responses to the following questions.

1. How do you feel about your progress on these goals at this point in time?

2. Please explain why you feel these goals were appropriately challenging, unrealistically challenging, or under-challenging.

3. What do you feel has been your greatest success this year?

4. What has been your biggest challenge?

5. What do you need from me as your supervisor to help you feel more successful in your current job?

II. 360 Feedback for Annual Review

(To be completed by teammates, direct reports, and others who are familiar with the individual's work.)

Thank you for completing the following questionnaire to assist me as I prepare for (Name of person being evaluated)_____'s annual feedback dialogue. Your responses will be compiled with those of other respondents to share with (Name)_____ and will remain as anonymous as possible. (The origin of some comments might be obvious based on content, but the author will not be revealed by me.)

DO NOT FEEL OBLIGATED TO COMMENT ON EVERY ITEM if there are any areas you have not observed or have no input to offer.

Please return your completed questionnaire to be me by (Date)_____ .

Thank you for your valuable input!

Name of person being evaluated:

_____

Your relation to this person (direct report, peer, colleague, friend, other:

_____

_____ I do not know this person well enough to offer any feedback at this time.

1. **Character/integrity** (reflects the character of Christ through 1) purity of heart, mind, and hands; 2) posture of servanthood; 3) perseverance; 4) trustworthiness; 5) promises kept and confidences held; 6) family life; 7) prayer; and 8) passion for Christ.)

   This person should continue...
   (How is the character of Christ reflected in their daily life?)

   This person should stop or needs improvement...
   (Are there any character flaws or blind sides that should be brought to their attention?)

   This person should start...
   (Are there any suggestions that would help this person grow in their character?)

2. **Interpersonal Relationships** (builds trust in others, demonstrates healthy one-on-one relationships)

   This person should continue...
   (What does this person do to encourage others or make others around them feel valued?)

This person should stop...
(Is there anything inappropriate or awkward in their
behavior toward others that might make others around
them feel uncomfortable?)

This person should start...
(Is there anything that could help this person improve
in their interpersonal relationships with others in their
work environment?)

3. **Time management/Getting things
   done** (organizes their daily and weekly activities, using
   their time productively to accomplish their goals)

   This person should continue...

   This person should stop...
   (Are there any current activities that this person could
   give up in order to make their time and/or the time of
   others around them more productive?)

   This person should start...
   (Is there something that could help this person
   improve the use of their time?

4. **Delegating appropriately to others** (not just
   "dumping" unwanted tasks)

   This person should continue...

   This person should stop or needs improvement...

   This person should start...

5. **Dealing with challenges/opposition** (How does this person handle stress, criticism, confrontation, and conflict management/resolution)

This person should continue...

This person should stop or needs improvement...

This person should start...

6. **Money management/handling budgets** (How well does this person understand the budgeting process? How well does he/she manage both personal and work finances?)

This person should continue...

This person should stop or needs improvement...

This person should start...

7. **Organizational alignment** (How well does this person understand the vision, mission and values of the organization? Do they make plans and set Specific, Measurable, Strategic goals that contribute to reaching the vision? Do they contribute to team-building?)

This person should continue...

This person should stop or needs improvement...

This person should start...

8. **Receiving direction** (How does this person respond to those in authority over them?)

This person should continue...

This person should stop or needs improvement...

This person should start...

9. **Leadership potential** (How would you rate this person's potential for advancement/promotion?)

10. **Additional comments** (Please share any additional suggestions that might help this person grow in their personal leadership development.)

III. Supervisor feedback
(Any additional comments)

Confronting for Change—Step by Step

The following seven-step approach outlines specific steps to take when confronting for change. This step-by-step approach follows the principles mentioned in the chapter on "Confronting for Change."

Step 1. PRAY

Step 2. Consult Up Line – Plan Your Action

- o In all cases it is good to give the next level of leadership a "heads up" that you are dealing with a personnel issue. Your leader may want to give counsel on how he wants you to proceed. Some leaders will give much more latitude while others will give specific guidance.

- o In cases of sexual misconduct, accusations of sexual misconduct, or intent to harm self or others, contact the appropriate leadership immediately. Specific steps must be taken according to policy and law. (Subsequent steps assume there is no sexual misconduct or intent to harm).

- o If the behavior might involve career-threatening behavior (other than sexual misconduct or intent to harm), it is especially important to alert the next level of leadership in case there are any policy-dictated procedures to follow. If the behavior involves any terminable offense, it is imperative that you contact the appropriate leadership immediately.

- o Be sure you and your supervisor are in agreement on the parameters of your authority to deal with the

249

problem. In most organizations, your supervisor and HR department must be contacted if you are desiring to do a formal corrective action involving a first or final warning or a termination.

o We strongly advise having a third person present. **NEVER confront a person of the opposite sex alone.**

o **Pray** for clear direction.

o Be sure to document the consultation for the file.

Step 3. Clarify Expectations – Ask, Listen, Talk, Listen, Write.

o As soon as you become aware of the problem, **confront in person** if at all possible. If not, use a telephone call or video conference. Never confront initially by email or snail mail.

o **Ask** questions to be sure your impressions and information are correct.

o Confront the individual **with gentle encouragement**. Let them know that you have their best interests at heart and want then to succeed.

o **Clearly describe** the expected behavior, attitude, or performance that is not being demonstrated as well as the unacceptable behavior or attitude, how it is adversely affecting the work and why it is unacceptable.

○ **Be specific** about the change in behavior that is required. Describe the following in specific language:

- how the behavior or attitude must change,
- what the new behavior or attitude will look like
- what time frame the change in behavior or attitude must take place.

○ **Explore** why the behavior or attitude is taking place. **Ask** questions and **LISTEN**. Be alert to the possibility that there may be a misperception of what is going on that needs to be clarified. Is the person aware of the expectations? Has adequate training been provided?

○ **Consider** if the problem might be a mismatch of the person's gifts and skills with the job. A change in jobs or job description might be in order.

○ **Offer assistance.** Help them write their own action plan, making sure the plan addresses the specific behavior or attitude that must change. Does the individual need a coach? Is an accountability partner needed? Would some special training help? Can you suggest a book? Is this an issue that should be referred to a counselor?

○ **Clarify** how progress will be reported and how often.

○ **Set a date and time** for a follow-up communication.

○ **Pray** with the individual to close the conversation.

○ BE SURE TO **DOCUMENT** THE EXPECTATIONS WITH A SUMMARY IN WRITING AND CONFIRM IN WRITING **TO THE INDIVIDUAL**. Ask the individual to respond in writing acknowledging receipt of the correspondence. Copy the correspondence to the file of record.

Step 4. First Follow up Meeting

- o **Recap** the expectations and refer to the follow up document.

- o **Ask** how the person thinks things have been going in this area.

- o If there has been any measure of progress toward a change, **CELEBRATE THE SMALL STEPS**.

- o If change has not been acceptable, **explain** that this is becoming a serious problem that must be addressed.

- o **Ask** what obstacles the individual is facing that might be preventing them from meeting the expectations that have been outlined previously.

- o **Explore** more possibilities of help that can be offered.

- o Set a specific date by which time the specific change in behavior must take place.

- o **Pray** with the individual to close the conversation.

- o BE SURE TO **DOCUMENT** THE WARNING AND ADDITIONAL STEPS TAKEN TO HELP THE INDIVIDUAL MAKE THE EXPECTED CHANGE. SUMMARIZE THE MEETING IN WRITING AND CONFIRM IN WRITING **TO THE INDIVIDUAL**. Ask the individual to respond in writing acknowledging receipt of the correspondence. Copy the correspondence to the file of record.

Step 5.   Second Follow up Meeting (if needed to address the same issues)

o   Again, this meeting should be made in person if at all possible, especially if the behavior might be leading to career-threatening action.

o   If the behavior has been corrected, be sure to **praise the improvement** (don't go overboard) and note the improvement in writing as well. "*If he listens to you, you have won your brother over.*" (Mt. 18:15) Talk through what the person has thought or done differently that has brought about the change and encourage them to continue improving in the problem area.

o   If the behavior has not changed, **issue a strong warning** (without being mean). Remind them of what was communicated earlier in the previous follow up time. **ASK and LISTEN**. Explore what has not worked and why the behavior has not changed.

o   If the behavior is causing serious damage to relationships or impeding the work of the individual or others around them, **point out that this appears to be a pattern of unacceptable behavior** (two points establish a line). Ask them if they can see that this does not seem to be working out.

o   Point out that it is unacceptable for this pattern to continue and failure to change will necessitate administrative action. **Communicate clearly the consequences of failure to correct the**

unacceptable behavior within a specified time. (This will likely include involving the next level of leadership and a formal corrective action process.)

- o **Explore** if any new action needs to be taken to get help.

- o **Establish a timeline for change.** The time should not be very long, but long enough to allow for observable change.

- o **Pray** with the individual to close the conversation.

- o **DOCUMENT.** Never leave a warning in the file without documentation of a follow-up!

Step 6. Follow Up in Writing and Inform Up Line

- o Be sure to follow up in writing and copy the next level of leadership. Ask the individual to respond in writing that they have received the correspondence and what is their commitment to make sure the unacceptable behavior does not continue.

- o In a separate report, document up line to the next level of leadership including a chronology of when the problem began, when and what actions have been taken, and the deadline given for the behavior to be corrected. Be sure copies of all the related correspondence are in the office of record.

Step 7. Take administrative action.

- o If the behavior persists to this point, action must be taken. Contact your supervisor and/or HR department to determine if a formal first warning or final warning corrective action is warranted. If that is the course of action, your HR representative will walk you through the steps for this to happen. You will definitely need to have a third person present when administrative action is being taken

o **Avoid the temptation to transfer problems to another assignment**. Only in rare cases should an individual be transferred while they are having problems that are affecting performance. If there is a clear mismatch of job assignment and the person could do another job that is truly needed, then explore that possibility. In most cases, the individual should demonstrate that the unacceptable behavior has been corrected first and then talk about a possible transfer.

In case of termination.

o If the administrative action leads to termination, this will be communicated by specific individuals according to policy. **Consult with your leader and HR representative** to be sure the appropriate procedures are followed.

o Be sure all levels of leadership up line are kept informed. Your leader should not be blindsided when questions arise or an appeal is made.

About the Authors

Larry and Susan Gay have over 35 years of experience in cross-cultural communication and leadership roles and have lived in Venezuela, Mexico, Ecuador, Cambodia, and Singapore. Larry is now an independent consultant and leadership coach working with business and ministry leaders in the USA and cross-cultural settings. Susan serves as a counselor and consultant to assess emotional wellness for potential expatriate employees.

Both Larry and Susan are Master Certified Professionals with The Birkman Method and Birkman Authorized Trainers. Since 2005, they have served as trainers of coaches with Grip-Birkman, a community of Christian coaches from a wide variety of denominations, churches, and organizations. Together they provide training in areas such as leadership development, healthy teaming, interpersonal skills, supervision, mentoring, conflict management, and marital and family health.

Larry has the Doctor of Educational Ministry degree from New Orleans Baptist Theological Seminary with a focus on strategic planning and leadership. Susan holds the Master of Arts in Marriage and Family Counseling from New Orleans Baptist Theological Seminary.

The Gays have three grown sons, two daughters by marriage, and three grandchildren: Andrew, Eden, and Matthew. They live in Montgomery, Alabama and can be contacted at LEAD360@gmail.com.

END NOTES

[1] Henry T. Blackaby and Richard Blackaby, *Spiritual Leadership: Moving People on to God's Agenda,* (Nashville: Broadman and Holman Publishers, 2001), 230.

[2] Blackaby, 231.

[3] Blackaby, 105.

[4] James M. Kouzes and Barry Z. Posner, *Credibility: How Leaders Gain and Lose it, Why People Demand It,* (San Francisco: Jossey-Bass Publishers, 1993), 22.

[5] Henry and Richard Blackaby agree that sexual sin is one of the most notorious pitfalls of leaders, 237.

[6] John Maxwell, *The 21 Irrefutable Laws of Leadership: Follow Them and People Will Follow You,* (Nashville: Thomas Nelson, 1998 and 2007)), 127.

[7] Ford, Dr. Paul R.. Moving from I to We: Recovering the Biblical Vision for Stewarding the Church (Kindle Locations 273-275). NavPress. Kindle Edition.

[8] Richard A. Swenson, *Margin: Restoring Emotional, Physical, Financial, and Time Reserves to Overloaded Lives,* (Colorado Springs: Navpress, 1992), 30-35.

[9] Swenson, 74.

[10] Swenson, 100.

[11] Swenson, 99.

[12] Swenson, 220.

[13] It would be great to get to the 80% suggested by the Pareto Principle. For more on the Pareto Principle, see http://www.pinnicle.com/Articles/Pareto_Principle/pareto_principle.html

[14] For more hints to leaders and followers, see Larry's occasional blog, "Lessons in Leadership and Followership" at http://mylead360.blogspot.com. Comments are welcomed or write to the authors at LEAD360@gmail.com.

[15] Marcus Buckingham and Curt Coffman, *First Break All the Rules: What the Worlds' Greatest Managers Do Differently,* (The Gallup Organization, 1999 and 2016), 33. They first stated what has now become the well-known maxim: "People leave managers, not companies."

[16] Doran C. McCarty first introduced the concept of adapting supervision to stages of development and need in his book, *Supervising Ministry Students* (Atlanta: Home Mission Board, SBC, 1978). McCarty's model is similar to Ken Blanchard's Situational Leadership model and was developed independently in the 1970's. McCarty's "States of Supervision" model also appears in a later publication, *SUPER-VISION: Developing and Directing People in Ministry* (St. Augustine, FL: McCarty Services, Inc., 2001), p. 55-60.

[17] We were serving with IMB, perhaps one of the largest conservative evangelical supervisory systems in the U.S.A. At that time, IMB had over 5,000 personnel—with 298 assigned to the Western South America Region that included Ecuador, Bolivia, Peru, Chile and Argentina.

[18] For more information about The Birkman Method, see www.Birkman.com/.

[19] For more information about Grip-Birkman, see www.GripBirkman.com/.

[20] Thanks to Shannon Ford and Mick Stockwell for introducing me to SMS goals as a substitute for SMART Goals. SMART can stand for specific, measurable, attainable, relevant and timely (or time-bound).

[21] The Birkman Method measures ten general categories of Interests. For more information see www.Birkman.com and www.GripBirkman.com. We will also address more about Interests in the chapter on "Teaming for Unity."

[22] *"Hablando, se entiende la gente."* Literally, "Talking, the people understand." This is a common saying in Mexico and other Spanish speaking cultures.

[23] As mentioned in the chapter on "Supervising for Success", all of these are addressed in The Birkman Method®, www.Birkman.com.

[24] We have some very simple tools for writing a personal mission statement that we often use in a half-day workshop. Contact the authors for more information at LEAD360@gmail.com.)

[25] We recommend *Your Leadership Grip,* as mentioned in the chapter on "Supervising for Success," www.GripBirkman.com.

[26] John Whitmore, *Coaching for Performance,* (Yarmouth, Maine: Nicholas Brealey Publishing, revised 2009). The book includes a more extensive list of potential questions in each of the four categories (Goal, Reality, Options and Will).

[27] For more information on their coaching model, see CoachWorks, International, https://www.coachworks.com.

[28] One of the best diagrams we have seen that illustrates this was a Transformational Leadership Model shared by Lee Ross in the early days of *Lead Like Jesus* Encounters sponsored by The Center for Faithwalk Leadership, Inc., a non-profit organization founded by Ken Blanchard and Phil Hodges. The original model Lee Ross used demonstrated a cyclical four-stage process to get to the desired effectiveness in the organization. The current version of *Lead Like Jesus* uses the same basic concepts in concentric circles and is titled "Spheres of Influence." For more information on the current *Lead Like Jesus,* see https://www.leadlikejesus.com/

Stephen Covey described the same basic principles using concentric circles in his book, *Principle-Centered Leadership,* (New York: Simon and Shuster, 1990).

[29] Stephen Covey, *Principle-Centered Leadership,* (New York: Simon and Shuster, 1990).

[30] For more information about The Birkman Method, see www.Birkman.com/.

[31] For more information about Grip-Birkman, see www.GripBirkman.com/.

[32] For more information about Style Matters, see www.riverhouseepress.com/.

[33] Adapted from Rob Wormley, "25 Employee Incentive Ideas That Won't Break The Bank," When I Work, Inc., Mar. 31, 2016, https://wheniwork.com/blog/employee-incentive-ideas/ (accessed on Oct 30, 2019).

[34] Ford, *Moving from I to We*, (Kindle Location 1361).

[35] Exodus 5.

[36] Dictionary.com

[37] (inspired by Patrick Lencioni, *Virtual Teams*, February 2009, http://www.tablegroup.com/blog/virtual-teams accessed Aug 17, 2015.)

[38] Rick Lepsinger, "Virtual Team Failure: Six Common Reasons Why Virtual Teams Do Not Succeed," http://www.businessknowhow.com/manage/virtualteam.htm , accessed August 18, 2015 and July 22, 2019. The article summarizes some of the conclusions from Lepsinger and De Rosa's book, *Virtual Team Success: A Practical Guide for Working and Leading from a Distance*, Jossey-Bass/A Wiley Imprint, 2010.

[39] Michael Hyatt has a very good article on "Over-Communicating" at https://michaelhyatt.com/leaders-communicate/.

[40] A great scene from the movie *Saving Private Ryan* is when Captain Miller responds to a question about his opinion on the wisdom of his squad's mission: "I don't gripe to you, Reiben. I'm a Captain. We have a chain of command. Gripes go up, not down. Always up. You gripe to me, I gripe to my superior officer, and so on and so on and so on. I don't gripe to you. I don't gripe in front of you. You should know that, as a Ranger."

[41] An online search will produce many helps for improving Emotional Intelligence. Daniel Goleman popularized the concept of EI in the mid-1990s with his

book, *Emotional Intelligence - Why it can matter more than IQ,* Bantam Books, 1996. Goleman refined the concepts and offered more practical applications for leadership and organizational change in his *Primal Leadership: Realizing the Power of Emotional Intelligence,* Harvard Business School Press, 2002.)

[42] *Diagnostic and Statistical Manual of Mental Disorders, 5th Edition (DSM-V)* is a manual published by the American Psychiatric Association (APA) that includes all currently recognized mental health disorders.

[43] Alvin Toffler, *Future Shock* (Random House, 1970).

[44] Daryl R. Conner, *Managing at the Speed of Change: How Resilient Managers Succeed and Prosper Where Others Fail* (Villard Books, 1993).

[45] Contact the authors for more information about writing your personal mission statement (LEAD360@gmail.com).

[46] Rick Warren, *The Purpose Driven Life: What on Earth Am I Here For?* (Zondervan, 2002), 21.

[47] Peter Senge, *The Fifth Discipline* (Doubleday, 1990). A plethora of books, essays and articles have addressed the need for any organization to have clearly stated vision, purpose and values. Of all these, Peter Senge's book *The Fifth Discipline* is still a seminal work for understanding systems thinking and how the pillars of vision, purpose and values work together within an organization.

[48] Ella Wheeler Wilcox, "'Tis the Set of the Sail —or— One Ship Sails East."

[49] William C. Byham, *Zapp! The Lightning of Empowerment: How to Improve Productivity, Quality, and Employee Satisfaction,* (Ballantine Books, 1997). In allegorical form, Byham demonstrated the effects of "Sapps" and "Zapps" to encourage or discourage morale and individual productivity.

[50] Leith Anderson, *Dying for Change* (Bethany House, 1998), 160.

51 David Augsburger, *Caring Enough to Confront* (Ventura, CA: Regals Books, 1986), 6, 11.

52 Ron Kraybill's *Style Matters* is available at http://www.riverhouseepress.com/.

53 Leith Anderson, *Dying for Change,* (Bethany House, 1998), 160. (It bears repeating!)

54 Ken Sande, *The Peacemaker,* (Grand Rapids: Baker Books, 1991, 1997), 12.

55 Sande, 56.

56 Cornelius Plantinga, Jr., *Not the Way It's Supposed to Be: A Breviary of Sin,* (Grand Rapids: Eerdmans, 1995).

57 Norm Wakefield, *Solving Problems Before They Become Conflicts,* (Grand Rapids: Zondervan, 1987), 11.

58 Fisher, Ury and Patton, p. 22.

59 Fisher, Ury and Patton, p. 29.

60 Wakefield, 154.

61 Wakefield, 13.

62 The concept of the "Anger Train" was inspired by Dr. James Headrick (d. 2004), professor at New Orleans Baptist Theological Seminary.

63 Roger Fisher, William L. Ury, and Bruce Patton, ed., *Getting to Yes: Negotiating Agreement Without Giving In,* (New York: Penguin Books, 1981, 1991, 2011), 10-11.

64 John Ortberg, *Everybody's Normal Till You Get to Know Them,* (Grand Rapids: Zondervan, 2003).

65 Ortberg, 169.

66 Ortberg, 173.

67 Ortberg, 195.

68 Not his real name.

69 Sadly, this is a true story.

70 A great illustration of this is in Henry Cloud's *Integrity,* (Harper Collins, 2006). p.13ff.

71 Tom Peters, *Thriving on Chaos: Handbook for a Management Revolution,* (Alfred A. Knopf, 1987).

[72] Leith Anderson, *Dying for Change*, (Minneapolis: Bethany House, 1992).

[73] Names changed to protect the privacy of the individuals.

[74] Dr. John Townsend, *Who's Pushing Your Buttons, Handling the Difficult People,* (Thomas Nelson: Nashville, 2004).

[75] Townsend, 52.

[76] Much of the material in this article appears in the blog: "Lessons on Leadership and Followership" http://mylead360.blogspot.com/, © Dr. Larry N. Gay, 2008, revised June 201

[77] The group, which included Sam James, Lloyd Rodgers, Van Payne, Tom Williams, Dickie Nelson, Elbert Smith and Larry Gay, met weekly for twelve weeks to examine the three Pastoral Letters verse by verse.

Made in the USA
Coppell, TX
26 November 2019